BLACK ECONOMIC DEVELOPMENT

The American Assembly, *Columbia University*

BLACK ECONOMIC DEVELOPMENT

Prentice-Hall, Inc., *Englewood Cliffs, N.J.*
A SPECTRUM BOOK

 P–13–077651–3; C–13–077669–6. *Library of Congress Catalog Card Number 79–79442.*

Printed in the United States of America.

Current printing (last number):
10 9 8 7 6 5 4 3 2

PRENTICE-HALL INTERNATIONAL, INC. (*London*)

Preface

The papers in this volume were first used as background reading for the Thirty-fifth American Assembly which met at Arden House, Harriman, New York, April 24–27, 1969 to discuss *Black Economic Development.* They now appear for general readership and as background for additional Assemblies in the United States.

The views contained herein are those of the writers and not necessarily of The American Assembly, a non-partisan educational organization which takes no position on matters it presents for public discussion. Similarly The Ford Foundation, which generously supported the entire American Assembly program on this subject, is not to be associated with the opinions expressed in the chapters which follow.

Clifford C. Nelson
President
The American Assembly

Table of Contents

William F. Haddad and
*G. Douglas Pugh, Editors**

Introduction

Sitting quietly with friends in an Indiana restaurant during the 1968 Presidential campaign, Robert Kennedy summed up what had become a new awareness of the roots of urban unrest. "The problems of America," he said, "are not as simple as the differences between white men and black men. They are as complicated as the differences between rich men and poor men."

That awareness was slow in coming. It was not until the second year of the War on Poverty, 1965, that the emerging black leadership began to make itself heard and to alter the agenda that white America had designed to pull minority Americans out of poverty. It was the much criticized (and, to this day, little understood) community participation mandates of the Economic Opportunity Act that gave these new leaders a voice, along with their first real access to power. For

---

WILLIAM F. HADDAD *is board chairman and chief executive officer of U.S. Research and Development Corporation. He has been an award-winning reporter for the New York* Post *and the New York* Herald Tribune, *a founder and associate director of the Peace Corps, and assistant director and inspector general of the Office of Economic Opportunity. A member of the New York City Board of Education and co-publisher of the* Manhattan Tribune, *Mr. Haddad has written articles for* Harper's Magazine *and is the author, with Richard Goodwin, of* The Hidden Force.

G. DOUGLAS PUGH *is a program advisor of the social development department at The Ford Foundation. A former Commissioner of the Federal Mediation and Conciliation Service, Mr. Pugh has served as industrial relations director of the Urban League of Greater New York, personnel director of Trafalgar Hospital, and associate executive director of HARYOU-ACT, Inc.*

* Mr. David Gelman was assistant editor for this project. He is a vice president of U.S. Research & Development Corporation.

the first time they could operate without the intercession of white interpreters who invariably mis-interpreted their aims and needs. They alone had the raw experience of life in the ghetto. The War on Poverty spurred them to marshal their resources and set the priorities for social change. And before long they began to articulate—accurately, for the first time—the frustrations of a community that had as the only guarantee of its life cycle an assurance that the children of poverty would grow up to be the parents of poverty.

In the early days of the poverty wars, these leaders had accepted the traditional agenda for change: integration was the first step to education; education was the first step to job-readiness; an entry-level job was the first rung on the ladder to middle class affluence. But even in those days it was apparent that the agenda was not working.

Integrated education, in practice, proved to be a kind of tokenism; it was no guarantee of quality education. Entry-level jobs, in practice, carried no guarantee of upward mobility.

What did happen, however, was that opening up these new jobs became a partnership venture among idealistic young federal officials, the new black leaders and the newly concerned American businessman (an unlikely alliance that may yet have a profound effect on the social history of this nation). The black leaders quickly learned the vocabulary of the white businessman, and began to probe the sources of real power within a democratic society. Black leaders in the past had always sought their portion of political power to provide the leverage for social change. The new generation of leaders now perceived that political power was often a function of economic power. To be sure, while they were beginning to exercise a degree of political suasion within the urban cores, they were still excluded from the centers of economic power which held the key to swift and massive change in the ghettos.

Having arrived at this understanding, the black leaders, along with a relatively small group of enlightened businessmen and poverty officials, began to forge the broad new agenda of "Black Capitalism."

As the first chapters in this volume point out, the problems of black entrepreneurship are acute. An overwhelming number of small businesses fail on their shaky foundations and poor management. The most serious shortage in the business world is the shortage of capable managers. The supply of black managers is almost nil. Capital for black business is always short and difficult to come by, the more so in a tight money market. In any traditional view, equity investment in marginal businesses is an inadvisable use of capital, and even by the high-risk, high-gain standards of venture capital, the ghetto is scarcely seen as a promising locale for investment. Moreover, information about potential markets for black businesses is skimpy, at best.

And though these problems have been mounting for decades, government policy for dealing with them has remained at low-priority and often contradictory.

The complex world of business has several traditional points of entry and advancement: the university business school; the family-owned business; the corporate spin-off; the talented manager branching out on his own; the development of a small business into a large enterprise; the adequately financed new idea. By history, by custom, and by an economic order in which the comparative sprinkling of ghetto businesses are eighty per cent owned by outsiders, most of these traditional entries are firmly closed to blacks.

A profound effect of this history—one which became, in turn, a cause—was the black man's image of himself. In any realistic appraisal of where he could earn his livelihood, what sort of self-image, indeed, could the black man develop? He could not begin to think of himself as an entrepreneur because those who had gone before him were not entrepreneurs. Business, the poverty and failure of his surroundings constantly reminded him, was "not his bag." His elders were servants and laborers, his contemporaries were trucker's helpers and dishwashers. Sweat and toil were the black man's talents. That is what society stood ready to reward him for, and if he wanted to support his family that was the reward he sought. (The movies and television, which sometimes reflect reality more accurately than they intend to, helped to support this image of lowliness by seldom portraying Negroes except as porters, doormen, domestics, bootblacks. And though both have recently begun altering this stereotype, late show movies of the thirties and forties still project the harsh truth of black servitude.)

All this, as the first chapters point out, combined to create formidable barriers around the black community. Yet the present volume is concerned less with the past than with the future—with what one writer calls the black man's ability to "break out." Once the underlying problems can be isolated and understood, they can be attacked, as our second group of writers indicate.

In the short run, for example, they find the need for equity capital, for long-term, low-interest loans, for partnerships that would eventually leave the black man in control. There is the need for hard-headed identification of markets and potential, for the financial packaging of ideas. Most important of all, the writers agree, is the need to locate, train, and support black managers. And threaded through the entire effort is the need to blend the restricted use of government money with high-risk venture capital.

But there are other issues which emerge in this book, and they are the issues on which black enterprise must rise or fall. In 1968, the New York Urban Coalition brought together businessmen, bankers, and black leaders to work out a formula for cooperation. In the process, what surfaced as the major problem was how to utilize white experience without subverting black leadership or control. This is the central dilemma which comes up repeatedly in these pages.

The struggle for control has begun even before the partnership papers have been drafted. One writer sees it as an assertion of the Negro's inalienable right to determine his own destiny. Howard Samuels terms it "compensatory capitalism," an economic philosophy of atonement for centuries of deprivation. David Hertz calls it "bridging the gap," and Roy Innis calls it, by his own lights, "separatist economics,"—a "preferential manipulation of the economy" to create, in effect, a sheltered economy in the black community. Dunbar McLaurin and Cyril Tyson offer, in the GHEDIPLAN, their own version of how a sheltered, preferential ghetto economy might operate. John McClaughry analyzes the options open to President Richard Nixon for establishing black control of the ghettos in terms of the Community Self-Determination Bill. And Wright Elliot asks the inevitable, tough-minded question of what is to be gained by the white businessman who plunges into a relationship with a hostile black community which wants his assistance without his participation.

When this book was first discusssed, it was unanimously agreed the title should be "Black Capitalism." But as the authors met to discuss their chapters, they sensed a growing antipathy to the use of the term "capitalism." The black leaders soon made it clear that they rejected the term. Capitalism, they argued, had not worked to eliminate the problems of poverty in the midst of affluence; if it was a success for the white man, it was a failure for the blacks, and thus they could hardly be asked to credit the so-called capitalist way of doing things as a model for black economic development.

At times the discussions grew acrimonious. To some of the white participants it seemed the blacks were inadvertently embracing a concept of exploitative capitalism which had fallen into disrepute back at the turn of the century. In effect, they felt, black leaders were asking to be helped in an effort to exploit the white community as they themselves had been exploited—a compensatory capitalism with overtones of vengefulness. But the black spokesmen were not convinced this was the case; or if it was, then a more advanced concept of capitalism must evolve from their planning, they insisted.

Since most of the authors were also among the prime movers of the black capitalism effort, the discussions on the book eventually broadened into contemporary action. It soon became common agreement that the goal was not necessarily black capitalism—defined by some skeptics as the creation of a few black millionaires—but a comprehensive plan of economic development skewed to give the bypassed

American minorities special assistance in establishing businesses, forming capital-accumulating instruments, building a managerial class, and in realizing from all of this a substantial measure of social benefit to the ghettos.

Several chapters of the book discuss methods of bringing about these comprehensive advances. Lawrence Johnson and Wendell Smith describe some present programs for training black managers and propose a vigorous program of recruitment by industry beginning at the high school level as a realistic way to begin closing the management gap. Douglas Pugh gives close attention to the bonding problem, the principal stumbling block for black entrepreneurs in the construction trades. Peter McNeish stresses the need for greater commitment and effort by banks and lending institutions. Martin Skala details some of the cooperative efforts already underway, while Gerson Green and Geoffrey Faux analyze the processes by which community controlled black enterprise can bring about "real integration" and greater social benefits in the long run.

The basic disputes are by no means resolved; nor can any single forum hope to achieve such a settlement. There remains an obvious gulf, for instance, between Roy Innis who wants separate institutions totally controlled by blacks, and David Hertz who advocates a partnership theory; between Howard Samuels urging a voluntary shift to humane new lending concepts, and Cyril Tyson urging that the leverage of public investment funds be used to *force* such changes. And the current of mutual mistrust between white businessmen and black leaders runs subtly but unmistakably through several of the chapters.

Yet what is also unmistakable is the willing-and-ready attitude of the participants. Contrasted with the one-sidedness of the economic contest over a period of centuries, the present disagreements seem merely superficial, and to that extent this volume provides an accurate measure of the problems and potentialities of ghetto development.

Our own belief is that the black leaders, speaking as the symbol of all the poor of this country, have located the underground river of power within democratic society. They have set as a goal an economic revolution which could be as crucial for the balanced development of this nation as the civil rights revolution set in motion by the Supreme Court decisions outlawing segregation.

What is already happening in this country today is a redefining of capitalism to broaden its concept, its implementation and its responsibilities. A black economic revolution along the lines that begin to be drawn in this book would bring a new competitive vitality and sense of fair play into the economic mainstream. The economy might thus renew itself at a point where pessimistic observers have begun to fear the limits of expansion have been reached.

But in any moral view there are higher stakes than a nation's economy. The drafters of our Constitution were not market analysts, they were idealists seeking a body of principles that would leave anarchy the only alternative to a social order based on what is just and right. In our own time that is still the choice for we know now that unless the opportunities of a democratic society are fairly distributed the resulting discontents will pull that democracy apart.

John Z. DeLorean

1

The Problem

History: Freedom Without Liberty

The American spirit is defined in a body of beliefs we have held sacred throughout much of our history. Some of these beliefs were enumerated by Robert and Helen Lynd in their classic studies of *Middletown,* the prototype American heartland community of the 20's and 30's. Among them:

> That economic conditions are the result of a natural order of things;
> That hardship is a good teacher, and can help turn a man with "the stuff in him" into a success;
> That it is a man's own fault if he does not get ahead in life; and
> That "social welfare" comes of "individual initiative, hard work, and thrift."

One can see here the familiar outlines of laissez-faire rugged individualism, self-reliance—the very stuff the American Dream was made of, through more than a century of national growth. More than merely a formal ideology, these were our ineffaceable household articles of faith, even when the Great Depression had thrown millions of Americans upon the benevolence of federal assistance programs.

Yet in recent years, we have been forcibly reminded that there is a whole segment of our population which has been unable to share this durable common faith. Where the Negro is concerned:

JOHN Z. DELOREAN *is vice-president of General Motors and general manager of Chevrolet Motor Division. Formerly general manager of Pontiac Motor Division, Mr. DeLorean is a mechanical and automotive engineer credited with more than 200 patents and patent applications.*

The "natural" order of the economy leaves him always at the bottom;
There is little prospect of a just reward for initiative;
His inability to get ahead is chiefly the fault of discrimination; and
Hardship is not his teacher but his permanent lot.

That these things are so has been a rough pill for most Americans to swallow. For it attacks our American equation of success; indeed, it is as if we were being told, after all these years, that the principles underlying our national faith are somehow false.

But it is not the principles that are false; rather it is our assumption that these principles have been available to *all* Americans that is false. For individualism and self-reliance are not automatic facts of American life: they are *opportunities*. And it is precisely the *opportunity* to function as self-reliant individuals, responsible for their own fate, that has been unavailable to most Negroes.

Historically, white America's efforts to "liberate" the Negro have always been clouded by ambivalence. It was the French essayist, Alexis de Tocqueville, who first noted on a visit to America in 1835 that "the prejudice of race appears to be stronger in the states which have abolished slavery than in those where it still exists. . . ." The tendency in many states of the Midwest and Far West in fact was to prohibit slavery while at the same time passing harsh restrictive measures against freed Negroes. Typical of this duplicity, as one recent study of slavery notes, was the comment by an Oregon newspaper in 1857: "Oregon is a land for the white man. Refusing the toleration of Negroes in our midst as slaves, we rightly and for yet stronger reasons, prohibit them from coming among us as free Negro vagabonds." [1]

Among these "stronger reasons" was the prevalent fear that freed Negroes would compete with whites for jobs, ownership of enterprise, and property. The very war that Northerners were fighting over the issue of slavery in the South seemed to heighten these fears.

Before long, influential Northerners (including, by some accounts, President Lincoln himself) were taking steps to see that newly emancipated Negroes were "contained" in the South or even "deported" to colonies in the Caribbean. At no time, apparently, was emancipation for the Negro permitted to imply equality of opportunity.

The containment policy kept Negroes largely confined to Southern agrarian experience. When they finally began moving northward in the last great wave of rural migration—attracted by the welfare advantages of the Thirties and the war industry jobs of the Forties—they came with neither the tradition, the know-how, the resources,

[1] Cited by C. Vann Woodward in the *New York Review of Books,* February 27, 1969.

nor, in any real sense, the freedom to take their place in an industrialized economy.

And the containment persisted. In the ghettos to which Negroes were instantly shunted, other ethnic minorities had been entrenched for nearly fifty years. Over the course of the half century these minorities had built their own potent political base, they had forged free access to capital resources, acquired control of their own thriving businesses. As the new migrants moved in, they moved out, banging the ghetto doors shut behind them. The Negroes were left to fend for themselves, with none of the access or means of development the old minorities had enjoyed. What is more, the departed whites retained control of most of the businesses, the lending institutions and real estate of the ghetto.

So for the Negro the ghetto was no gateway to America as it had traditionally been for earlier arrivals; it was simply one more colony. The Negro owned none of its meager assets. He worked outside the ghetto in menial jobs, acquiring no management or entrepreneurial skills to bring back with him. What little capital he accumulated he expended outside the ghetto. For what little purchases he made within the ghetto, he paid higher prices, because of the relatively small volume of purchases and the high credit risk he carried. What little ability he had to pay rent and buy commodities was exploited by absentee white landlords and shopowners at the same time that they allowed his physical environment to decline to the point of ruin. Lenders and investors shunned him, and even his city government gave him the last and least of its services.

Statistics: The Size of the Problem

Today there are 21 million blacks in America, more than two-thirds of them living with the disproportionate arithmetic of the ghetto. Their income is half the national average; their unemployment, three times the national average. The rough-and-tumble of the urban economy has all but excluded them from the contest. Their current business history is written largely in marginally operative retail and service enterprises.

As reported in the *Christian Science Monitor,* a recent study by Wall Street investment banker Joseph M. Kirchheimer shows:

> The overwhelming majority of black business are individual proprietorships in the retailing and services sector. Most are 'Mom and Pop' stores, employing fewer than five people, and varying in value from $5,000 to $50,000. These stores consist mainly of eating places, beauty parlors, apparel, liquor, and second-hand shops. Such businesses are often very shaky. They rarely accumulate significant capital for their owners and have a high failure rate. . . .

. . . Mr. Kirchheimer's three-month investigation in major cities such as Los Angeles, St. Louis, and Minneapolis (and 10 other cities) leads to the conclusion that in many inner-city areas the attrition rate of black merchants exceeds the birthrate. He cites the problems of getting access to capital, developing competent entrepreneurs, and marrying these to viable opportunities as the 'chief constraints' on business progress.

Today there are only a relative handful of Negroes who can seriously be classified as businessmen. According to Dempsey J. Travis, president of an association of Negro mortgage bankers, there are fewer Negro businesses of significant size now than there were 40 years ago. Between 1950 and 1960, Negro business ownership actually declined 20 per cent while business ownership in the United States as a whole was increasing. Less than three per cent of all United States industry, less than two per cent of construction enterprises, less than one per cent of manfacturing, are minority-owned, and 73 per cent of the businesses Negroes do own is centered in the profitless barrens of the ghettos, catering to a segregated clientele.

The Council for Equal Business Opportunity reports that by some estimates, Negroes own around one-tenth the number of businesses they should own based on their percentage of the total population. The Kirchheimer study notes that in Newark, New Jersey, more than 50 per cent of the population is black, yet only a little over ten per cent of the approximately 12,200 licensed businesses are owned by blacks. In New York City, one out of every 1,000 blacks—as against one out of every 40 whites—owns a business of any kind.

Those are the bare measurements of the problem. Essentially, they describe the past, but they speak poorly for the immediate future as well. For if a black business class is to develop, it must virtually materialize out of thin air. Within the ghetto there are scarcely any models, any tradition, any experience—or, for that matter, any means—for it to draw on.

Breaking Out

In the modern era of the civil rights movement there are disturbing parallels to the ambivalent attitudes of a century ago. In recent years, attempts to help Negroes break the chains of the ghettos focused first on social service, health, and welfare assistance. These were essentially paternalistic measures, palliative rather than corrective, and under the benevolent tyranny of the welfare system the effect has often been to institutionalize the deficiencies it seeks to offset.

As the War on Poverty took on formal lines, the emphasis shifted to manpower employment programs. But these also fell far short of any realistic goals. For the most part, jobs for Negroes continued to be menial, dead-ended, with little opportunity for advancement. Moreover, government-supported manpower programs tended to "cream" the labor market, scarcely touching the hard-core depths of the chronically unemployed and under-employed.

In the meantime, Negro leaders were becoming increasingly skeptical of white intentions, while their followers grew increasingly frustrated and embittered at the failure of such measures to improve their condition. Many wondered whether they could ever expect more than "tokenism," from a white society seemingly bent on appeasing them without ever really helping them, and on offering them "equality" without opportunity. In truth, the attitudes of a great many whites remained as puzzling, as elusive as they had been a hundred years before. They professed, for example, to favor integration measures, yet they resisted open housing ordinances; they supported hiring of Negroes, yet opposed promotion of Negroes. They seemed to approve Negro equality in principle; in practice, it made them uneasy.

What white Americans were finally coming face to face with—what they had perhaps been seeking to avoid ever since the Civil War—was the necessity, at last, of permitting Negroes to become economically competitive, a far more challenging proposition than mere integration. Equal opportunity for Negroes, in short, meant the opportunity to succeed, or to fail, on the same terms that were available everywhere to whites. For their part, Negroes had come to realize that what they had truly been denied all these years was the right that free Americans profess to value above all others—the right to help themselves. More than integration, more than government benevolence, more than jobs, they wanted the right to control their own economic institutions, to generate their own jobs, their own capital, their own social programs—and thus to control their own destinies.

The idea was certainly not a revolutionary one, nor even strikingly new. Yet with the apparent bankruptcy of so many of the old approaches, with the volatile ghettos exploding summer after summer, suddenly the major emphasis of the civil rights movement in America has shifted to "black capitalism" as the means—perhaps only the latest means—of helping Negroes become more or less competitive in a capitalistic society. Basically, this envisages the development of black entrepreneurs on a major scale through a variety of approaches:

Branch operations of big industry in the inner city;

Indigenous inner-city industries assisted by partnership arrangements or by technical and managerial support from outside corporations;

Individually operated inner-city enterprises made possible through compensatory devices such as Small Business Administration loans, managerial and technical training programs, sheltered markets, etc.; and

Community-owned corporations financing local enterprise and social services.

The new strategy took root almost immediately on the civil rights staging grounds of the nation, gaining considerable momentum from Richard Nixon's "Bridges to Human Dignity" campaign speeches in the spring of 1968. Here, once again, is seen a way to justice—a way of equalizing the system after two centuries of gross disadvantage to the Negro, a way of reshaping the rules of the game no more unfairly than giving the perennially last place football club first draft choice.

Supporters of this concept cite the familiar arguments that a more productive ghetto means a greater GNP for the nation as a whole; greater tax revenues; reduction of welfare rolls; reduction of racial tension, unrest, and crime in the cities; expansion of the overall labor and management pool for American industry. But more important than income and jobs, they feel, black capitalism could at last begin to create the economic institutions, and thus the political institutions, that could begin to make the inner-city residents competitive on equal terms with white society.

Yet it is by no means a clear-cut concept, or one that can be certain in its effects, and it has already gathered around it enough equally convinced critics and proponents to launch a stormy new era of civil rights controversy.

The Hang-Ups

If we have learned nothing else from the past decade of racial turmoil, we should have learned at least that there is no single panacea for America's oldest and deadliest problem. The idea of black capitalism has been embraced all too eagerly by white planners who apparently see it as a way of regaining credibility in the ghettos. Yet the wounds of the black-white confrontation are by now too deep to permit any painless reconciliation. The white business community must accept, to begin with, that if it enters into a formal association with black entrepreneurs, it may be a relationship without affection, or worse, without trust, for some time to come. Whether business partners can profit or survive in a mutually abrasive climate is one of the major question marks for black capitalism. Yet paradoxically, it is one of the strengths of the concept; for that is the contest in which the black man, until now, has been denied a chance to play.

CONCEPTUAL PROBLEMS

Beyond that, the path to black capitalism is a rough one, pocked with philosophical and practical pitfalls. On the philosophical side, there are those who feel the problem should be approached as if the ghetto were an underdeveloped nation. That is, government and business forces should do everything in their power to establish within the ghetto a stable, self-sustaining economy that would foster a stable life in the community. Others point out that unlike the underdeveloped nation, the ghetto has only one indigenous resource—its own manpower—and this can be developed only if industry, materials, and capital are imported. This, they warn, would merely promote a new colonialism. Inevitably, outside investors would drain off profits, exploit indigenous labor and skills, while creating little capability in the community itself. Thus they insist on guarantees of early divestiture by outside partners, or better yet, complete internal control through community corporations, for example.

A third voice in the argument holds that an independent black economic system is neither feasible nor desirable. One spokesman for this point of view is Frederick Sturdivant, of the University of Texas Graduate School of Business. Writing in the *Harvard Business Review,* Sturdivant attacked the proposed Community Self-Determination Act, which guarantees community-owned corporations strong leverage over outside corporations doing business in the ghetto as well as over indigenous enterprises within the ghetto. The bill, he declares,

> ignores the great challenge that confronts this nation, which is to find ways to surmount the racial barriers erected by the dominant society and create a truly pluralistic democracy. Any legislation that ignores this objective and enforces a concept of 'separate but equal' economic development moves the nation toward apartheid. . . . If economic integration . . . is to be viewed as a step toward the goal of equal rights and opportunities for all citizens of this nation, then this approach to black capitalism is not the answer.

There is, in fact, a full range of black capitalism opinions with the issue of control constantly cropping up as the single thorniest item. It is in their utterances on control of black business that Negroes show how profound their mistrust of the white community has become. "Business for black people must include development of their self-awareness," said Mary Treadwell, program development director of Washington, D.C.'s Pride, Inc. "Everybody and his mother used to be able to come into black communities and operate, and whether they boycott or burn, people in black communities just aren't going to stand for that anymore."

Or consider such sentiments as the following:

> We have many analogies, from countries such as Jamaica for example, of the great dangers that arise when the business community comes in. In those places you now have a new black managerial class. . . . They pay for their new-found affluence by keeping order over the masses of black people who are not benefitting in any way from the development and

exploitation of the resources of that country. . . . We can expect the same thing here: The massive infusions of corporate investments in the ghetto will develop a new black managerial class that will have the responsibility for maintaining order over the masses of black people.

And from another participant:

By hook or crook, Bedford-Stuyvesant, Harlem and South Bronx [Negro sections of New York City] and all the black areas are going to be recaptured by whites—whether it is by the insurance companies in cahoots with the bankers or some other scheme. While they are placating us with little jobs here and there and arguing about who gets the directorship for this or the other program, they are getting ready to reclaim that land.

While these expressions represent the extreme of mistrust, they are by no means confined to extremists. This was no dialogue on a ghetto streetcorner, but rather a symposium of responsible black spokesmen conducted by *New Generations,* a publication of the National Committee on Employment of Youth. The message to the white business community is this: that even in black capitalism, the concept which professes to offer the ultimate concession of independence and self-determination to the ghetto, the black community sees the familiar spectre of white planning, white manipulation, and ultimately white control.

As one participant emphasized: "If black people don't own and control it [ghetto enterprise] the most important factor is lost. There are some gains, but not the ones we need most of all at this time—to make our own decisions and control our own lives."

It scarcely matters at this point whether such attitudes are warranted. What matters is that they exist, and must be dealt with, if the concept of black economic development is to be given a serious trial.

PRACTICAL PROBLEMS

It can be presumed that the philosophical differences on black capitalism are not irreconcilable; all points of view seem to accept the underlying principle of the need for ghetto economic development. The practical problems may be harder to resolve. Just as poverty itself has been a self-perpetuating cycle for the Negro, so has his record of business failure and frustration.

The building trades industry is a prime example. As G. Douglas Pugh points out in chapter 11, most of the 8,000 minority group contractors in the nation have found it next to impossible to obtain the surety bonds without which they cannot obtain contract work—and the needed experience to assure them future work. In a statement to the Small Business Administration in September of 1968, the American Insurance Association declared:

> As contractors, Negroes and other American minorities lack the necessary management and technical skills, experience and financial capacity. As a result, they operate at a low level of efficiency, organization and profitability.

A typical encounter has been described elsewhere by Cyril Tyson, one of the contributors to this volume:

> We talked to the Mayor of Baltimore about a piece of the Model Cities action. We are talking about who is going to reconstruct the buildings recently damaged [in the Baltimore ghetto disorders]. But the first question we got back is, 'Who have you got that can really do the job?' Now that's a sensible question. But at the same time you can't expect qualified Negroes to suddenly bloom out of the ghetto when they haven't had a chance for generations.

The "action" Tyson refers to is considerable, and not just in Model Cities programs. In all there is $100 billion spent in construction each year in the United States, and the Negro contractor's share of this is miniscule, even in the business of renovating his own community.

A study by New York's Economic Development Task Force underscored the general difficulties for black entrepreneurs:

> Because minority businessmen have participated primarily in small business ventures, a high proportion of which have been unsuccessful, they have been unable to survive their mistakes and thus gain business experience.

Minority businessmen, the report continues, lack know-how in "such basic functions as administering day-to-day operations, planning and controlling finances, marketing, purchasing and controlling inventory." All of this, the study adds, contributes to a high rate of failure and also makes the black entrepreneur

> a poor risk in the eyes of the traditional investor. Financing is extremely scarce. There is virtually no source of venture capital; short-term and long-term low-interest loans are in critically short supply; and organizations willing and able to invest in existing and new ghetto enterprises are few and far between.
>
> Many minority businessmen must use a middleman to purchase inventory, because they cannot establish sufficient credit or finance a large enough inventory to qualify for volume discounts.

Banks and lending institutions have come in for their share of criticism from struggling black entrepreneurs. Negro contractors, for example, complain that without sufficient assets they cannot obtain loans; yet without loans, they cannot get sufficient working capital to build their assets. "We have the experience and the enthusiasm to make a dent in the housing shortage and the many thousands of substandard homes," says George Walker, head of an association of black building contractors in Detroit. "But most black contractors start out very small and are inadequately financed. A banker will automatically shake his head and say a black contractor is a bad risk."

Under the circumstances, black-owned banks might be expected to play a crucial role. Today, however, there are only 20 Negro-owned banks operating in 19 cities in the nation, a significant decline from the total of 49 in 38 cities back in 1929. According to Andrew F. Brimmer (the only Negro member of the Federal Reserve Board), owing to the "adverse loan experience" of these banks, "as a group [they] have had no after-tax profits during the last three years [1965–1968]." Part of the difficulty, he added, is "that the market for their services is circumscribed by the general conditions in the ghetto—high unemployment, low incomes, a low rate of savings and the marginal character of local businesses. These obstacles are reinforced by the severe shortage of trained management personnel."

If the prospect for Negro-owned banks is dim, there are those who find little but gloom in the outlook for major black enterprise in general. In the *Harvard Business Review,* John T. Garrity, an officer of McKinsey & Company, Inc., drew up an outline for the operations of a hypothetical "Ghetto Manufacturing Company," comparing it with the operations of "Typical Industries, Inc." a hypothetical white-owned corporation. The balance sheet is anything but encouraging. Turnover, training costs, and hiring costs at Ghetto Mfg. are all far higher than those at Typical. As a result,

> Ghetto Manufacturing loses more than $1,000,000 in its first year. The subsequent average annual after-tax profit of approximately $30,000 does not cover this initial loss, and the cumulative loss is about $650,000. . . . Thus, because of its $3,400,000 higher labor turnover cost, Ghetto Manufacturing over the ten years goes nearly $600,000 into the red, as compared with Typical Industries' ten-year pretax profit of more than $3,000,000.

Needed: Creative Solutions

For better or worse, Negroes want their own share in the American system. They do not want white economists or social planners determining what is best for them. They want the chance to succeed or fail on their own terms, on their own responsibility, in their own enterprises. As the Reverend Leon H. Sullivan, a promoter of large scale black business ventures succinctly stated, in an interview with *U S News and World Report,* "A man is not free until he owns something and has self-pride."

Black and white business analysts can at least agree on an order of priorities for ghetto economic development. The imperatives are these:

Locate capable black businessmen;
Liberalize concepts and standards of lending, bonding, and insurance;
Provide managerial training, technical assistance, and support, identify viable markets; and
Provide easier access to markets for minority entrepreneurs. If necessary, provide sheltered markets.

No matter the obstacles, the Reverend Sullivan (whose successes are described by Martin Skala in chapter 12 of this volume) has great expectations for the future. "It is my hope," he told *U S News and World Report,* "that by the year 2000 at least 100,000 new businesses will have been created by blacks—selling or making things for the total American community. By that time, I hope, these establishments will be employing 5 million people and generating 50 billion dollars in new wealth."

The Small Business Administration, rooted in the realities of the present, more modestly hopes to double the existing number of minority-owned businesses by 1975. Says an agency report,

> Our analysis recognizes that greatest opportunities will arise in the retail trade and service industries, but contemplates principal expansion in the more substantial segments of these industries [shopping centers, franchises, supermarkets, business, professional, and technical services]. It also proposes progressive growth of minority ownership in other industries, especially in contract construction, but also in wholesale trade and manufacturing.

To point the way for black and white communities to work together for ghetto economic development, there are few better examples than the New York Urban Coalition. With the help of a committee of bankers, the Coalition formed a non-profit corporation with three planned subsidiary operations.

The first would utilize the government leverage possible in the Small Business Investment Company Act. Because this mode of government support is restrictive, the Coalition also would establish a Venture Capital Corporation to finance businesses which are potentially successful but entail a greater risk factor. The final subsidiary would provide management assistance to the ghetto areas of the city. It would help to define local business opportunities, help to find potential managers and owners, establish apprenticeship programs to train them, and package the investment for consideration by traditional banking sources or the Venture Capital Corporation. The Board of Directors would be broadly based, with adequate representation of both the financial institutions and the community leaders, but in no case of a quality and experience below that of a comparable bank board.

A number of government assistance programs have either been proposed or are already underway. The SBA has black entrepreneurship teams promoting black business in upwards of 40 cities throughout the country. The agency also has proposed tripling SBA loans to ghetto business, under liberalized lending concepts, and SBA's Project OWN is promoting bank credit for minority entrepreneurs with a system of government guarantees. The Federal Task Force on Urban Problems has proposed an urban development bank to finance ghetto business projects with low cost loans, as the World Bank does for underdeveloped nations.

A growing number of private organizations operated by blacks, such as NEGRO and the Reverend Sullivan's OICs (Opportunities Industrialization Centers) are helping to launch, finance, or staff black business enterprises.

There seems, on the whole, no lack of piecemeal efforts scattered throughout the states. One reads, for example, of idealistically committed young bankers and business executives providing voluntary advice and assistance to ghetto entrepreneurs; of associations of black churchmen raising funds from parishioners to promote businesses; of a Ford Foundation grant of $300,000 to help fund minority contractors; of individual business firms, trade associations, franchisors, professional associations and the like making special efforts to assist ghetto business.

Many observers have warned, however, that piecemeal efforts will make no appreciable dent in the problem and may merely add up to one more prolonged experience of failure for the Negro. "These efforts, thus far, have been highly diffused and uncoordinated," says the SBA. Through Project OWN, the agency hopes to provide a focal point for the coordination of such assistance at the community level. The ambitious Community Self-Determination Act, which authorizes the establishment of federally chartered development corporations in ghetto communities of up to 300,000 population (details appear in chapters 3 and 4), is an attempt to institutionalize black enterprise as a community-wide cooperative venture. (The quasi-dictatorial controls and sanctions over local businessmen that this would place in the hands of the community corporations are a subject of heated debate among business experts.)

All in all, the next attempt to bridge the racial gap in America is beginning to coalesce. Yet what is still vitally lacking is the force of a major commitment, the sort of vast and sudden accretion of energy, effort, and inventiveness that turned us into an awesome military power virtually overnight in World War II, or thrust us dramatically ahead in the space race in this decade. When our goal has been clear and our motivation intense we have demonstrated the power to reshape events and control our destiny.

There would seem no less urgency in the challenge of black economic development. Yet the responses remain mixed. Here and there, creative solutions come forth: an eight-bank credit-guaranty pool is formed in Philadelphia to channel capital into the inner city; a private and federally funded Restoration Corporation (organized by the late Senator Robert Kennedy) undertakes the rehabilitation of a vast Brooklyn slum; the Nixon administration appears ready to support legislation for a national community development bank. But on the other hand, business as a whole approaches the problem as mistrustfully as the ghetto inhabitants themselves; former SBA director Howard Samuels notes that major auto and appliance franchisers are reluctant to promote black franchises because of the unlikelihood of substantial revenue in the ghettos in the near future.

So it may be that business motivation will have to be stimulated with tax incentives and other artificial inducements. And certainly, the ghetto will have to overcome its own hang-ups about accepting advice, assistance, and support from the white business community.

No instant miracles of change can be expected from this shotgun marriage. Americans grew sadder in the late 1960s, but also wiser. They know now that there is no single solution to the massive problems of the ghettos. Black economic development is a treatment, not to be mistaken for a cure. As a request from the ghettos, it is still evolving. Other treatments have been in progress for years, and may be equally useful. But if the methods are still being formulated, the goals should be as singular and clear as a wartime victory or a landing on the moon:

The Negro wants the right to determine his own destiny. That is the right we promote in Latin America, in Eastern Europe, in Africa. It is ostensibly the right we have been fighting for in Vietnam, and for whose defense we continue to build missile systems and to stockpile nuclear weaponry.

At the very least, then, we owe this right of self-determination to the fellow Americans in our own ghettos. If it appears at first to lead to separatism, to an uneasy co-existence, that may be a chance we must take, just as we do when we uphold the right of an uncommitted nation to conduct free elections. In the long run, it is perhaps the only way of retaining the trust of 21 million black Americans, with whom we can strive toward an economic order in which the contest is equal and there is competition without strife.

Gerson Green and Geoffrey Faux

2

The Social Utility of Black Enterprise

"Green Power" movements have been developing among minority groups at a very rapid pace over the past two years causing government, foundations, and the business leadership to grope for policy and program guidelines.

Although there is general agreement that the development of black enterprise efforts is necessary and desirable, there is little actual program experience upon which to base judgments as to scale and type of programs. Most urban black enterprise projects are still in the development stage; few have been operational for more than two years.

Roughly the debates, both within the ghetto and without, fall into two schools. One school emphasizes the cost side of the cost-benefit question, holding that the ghettos present the least fruitful areas for enterprise development, in that land, facility, and maintenance costs are exceedingly high, circulation is congested, housing amenities and transportation are inadequate, crime and hostility in the ghettos prevent the employment of competent management and clerical staffs, and insurance costs are excessive. This argument represents the majority view in government and business, and has resulted in the almost sole dependence on employment programs supported by social services to achieve economic well-being in the ghetto.

The second school emphasizes the benefits, or social utility, side of the equation. It holds that the economic structure which puts the

GERSON GREEN *is director of the Research and Demonstration Division of the Community Action Program of the Office of Economic Opportunity.* GEOFFREY FAUX *is chief of the Economic Development Branch of the Policy and Evaluation Division of the Community Action Program of the Office of Economic Opportunity.*

ghetto at a competitive disadvantage is not due to natural market forces but to specific resource allocation policies (highways, housing, tax policies) which have built up the infrastructure of the suburbs and small cities at the expense of the urban core. Those in this school will argue that our investment policies could and should be changed to aid ghetto areas and that, in effect, the "cost-effectiveness" position is another variant of "socialism for the rich, free enterprise for the poor." The need is to concentrate upon the social utility of the program, just as we emphasize the benefits of the defense, space, and highway programs, and rarely their costs.

These two views are complicated by the current clash of integrationist and separatist philosophies. In general the "cost effectives" hold the integrationist view that blacks can best assimilate into American life through opening up housing and jobs in suburban growth areas, and that the tools, legal and programmatic, are now at hand. The National Alliance of Businessmen proceeded on this view. The "social utilitarians" argue that recent data indicates a slight opening-up of the suburbs to blacks and that the trend will increase, but that such movement has affected only the black upper-middle class and has thus further reduced the leadership in the ghettos, leaving the great mass of blacks doomed to decades of existence in deteriorating neighborhoods. Black planners and architects are providing an additional view holding that if American cities are to survive as viable social systems, the ghettos must be made to flower into desirable total living environments. On this issue, the cost effectives argue that the function of the ghetto is a transition to assimilation into suburban life. This is a maintenance view leading to minimal investment in physical and economic development of the ghettos and stressing ameliorative social service and employment programs to help more residents up and out of the ghetto. The social utilitarians hold that the blacks now occupy prime land in our inner cities which will ultimately be reclaimed and rebuilt, and that large numbers of blacks should remain and benefit from the rebuilding. The current mood of the ghetto would appear to require a policy of rebuilding for current residents.

This represents, in crude form, the policy context from which our argument follows.

The Benefits

The War on Poverty (appropriations to the Economic Opportunity Act) currently costs some $2 billion per year. Over eight hundred millions are invested in OEO's Community Action Program, for both rural and urban areas, the heart of the self-help organizational effort in the ghettos. With the advent of the Model Cities Program, the urban areas may receive a significant increase in resources. Little, if any, of the current and projected resources are earmarked for the economic development of black ghettos, principally because government planners continue to place their main reliance on manpower training and social service programs.

The question of whether the economic development of poor ghetto areas should be an appropriate goal of federal anti-poverty policy usually dissolves into a simplistic comparison between "employment" programs and "investment" programs. The question is then posed, should we bring people to the jobs or the jobs to the people? From the outset, the focus is upon jobs and it is an easy step from there that jobs are the ultimate measure of program effectiveness.

Despite the fact that an investment program, the Area Redevelopment Act, was the first major new program established by the Kennedy Administration, for most of the sixties the argument has been carried by those supporting the "employment" or "manpower training" alternative. The debate, of course, has a history of its own. It has involved specific personalities and political relationships which themselves have had no small impact upon policy decisions. But the basic thrust of program analysis has consistently, almost exclusively, favored employment programs, implicitly concluding that either the costs of economic development were too high, the benefits too low, or both.

Even on its own terms (i.e., the primacy of the employment goal), the analysis upon which the conventional conclusion is based has not been very thorough. Comparative costs of employment and investment programs have not been established, and the variables of the employment goal (who is hired, what kinds of jobs, etc.) rarely isolated and tested separately. In addition, the variety of possibilities on the economic development side are almost never postulated. However, even if the techniques and data were available for making valid comparisons between training programs and economic development, the conceptual basis for making such comparisons would still be in error. Job training cannot be compared with economic development on an either/or basis, because job training programs have one single objective—employment—while economic development is a program with multiple objectives, one of which is employment. Thus the real issue is whether or not there should be an *exclusive* reliance upon manpower and other similar employment programs, or whether some mix of economic development and job training would be more cost effective in the long run.

Before addressing the basic issue, there should be an understanding of what is meant by economic development in the context of domestic urban problems. Terminology is a problem here. Clearly, we are not talking about economic development as the term is usually applied to underdeveloped nations; that is, the problem of increasing the output and productivity of the population of a large, more or less self-contained geographical unit, the solution to which involves the techniques and strategies of capital accumulation. While there are certain analogies between a ghetto community and an underdeveloped country, the analogy as an operating principle breaks down quickly, mostly because of the difficulties in defining the ghetto in economic terms and in identifying and controlling such economic indicators as imports and exports. The problem in our inner cities is somewhat different. It deals ultimately with the redistribution of income, employment, and ownership among income classes, and to a degree, among racial groups through the development of a business infrastructure in the ghetto itself.

Thus far there is no significant national program for this kind of economic development. Title IV of the Economic Opportunity Act, which provides loans and technical assistance to poverty area entrepreneurs, was an attempt to add a modest economic development dimension to the poverty program. It proved inadequate to the task for administrative reasons, and because of the concentration of effort on small high risk "Mom and Pop" stores. Recently, SBA has tried to move away from reliance on small marginal enterprises and may be having some effect upon improved access to capital and technical assistance by black and other minority businessmen. The Economic Development Administration operates what is essentially a rural area and small town program. It does have an urban technical assistance program which has engaged in some creative projects but that program has been limited both in money and program authority. OEO has funded several demonstration projects in this area, but thus far has not looked upon economic development as an area of major program interest.

The history of the Kennedy-Javits Amendment to the Economic Opportunity Act (described by Mr. Hertz in chapter 8), which calls for massive investment in poverty areas but has been assigned a miniscule role in the Poverty Program, is evidence that economic development has not been taken seriously as part of a total antipoverty strategy.

Thus those who argue for exclusive reliance upon employment programs have been in the ascendancy during the short history of the War on Poverty. The basic argument for this position centers around two propositions: 1) that employment programs at all times are more efficient in the development of jobs than investment programs; 2) that economic development programs will increase segregation and encourage separatism.

These points, as well as the identification of some additional social benefits of economic development are discussed below.

EMPLOYMENT

It should first be understood that the authors of this chapter do not believe that there is any realistic substitute for job training and related employment programs. The majority of the hard-core unemployed in our ghetto areas will find jobs located outside the ghetto. However, over the past few years a huge assortment of these programs have been funded. Some have succeeded; many have failed. While the failure of individual programs as a result of inadequate techniques or poor management does not necessarily mean that the strategy of training ghetto dwellers is wrong, it has brought the strategy of *exclusive* reliance upon such programs into serious question. Part of the problem lies in the basic assumption that any job paying something above subsistence is a sufficient inducement to the black ghetto dweller for him to travel long distances and subject himself to the psychological pressures attendant upon breaking into employment areas traditionally held by lower middle class whites. It is, of course, hard to say just how much of current chronic unemployment is a result of this problem. Estimates have been made but reliable information on the reasons for high failure rates of employment programs are simply not available. The reports of people running through training program after training program without ending up in a permanent job indicate that it is enough to be concerned about.

Certainly, part of the failure of conventional employment progress can be traced to technical and administrative problems rather than to the concept itself. Lack of experience in training the inner-city unemployed and sluggishness of institutions responsible for the programs have taken their toll. As experience accumulates, these problems should diminish.

Another part of the problem comes from a lack of sufficient demand for unskilled and semiskilled labor at the upper limits of acceptable price increase in the economy, which thus creates a pool of unemployed workers at any given period of time.

However, a third reason for the continued existence of so many hard-core unemployed certainly is an insufficient understanding and appreciation of the race problem in America. Consider the case of the "hard-core" young black male adult who successfully completes a training course and for whom a job is available (a situation which often does *not* result from training programs). So far his life has been one humiliating failure after another. As a result, he has little confidence in his ability to cope with the difficulties emanating from his being black and poor in a white middle class society. He gets his job as a result of a highly publicized employment program in his city, through which firms in the suburbs agree to make jobs available to black inner-city residents. He is thus greeted by a *white* personnel manager, a *white* foreman, and *white* co-workers. They resent the "special" treatment he is getting and they let him know it. The pressures on him to succeed become enormous, and in a few weeks he drops out. He adds another failure to his personal history and returns to the economically less satisfying but psychologically tolerable life on the streets. At the same time, the experience, repeated over and over, convinces the plant manager, the personnel manager, the foreman, and the white workers that "these people" just do not want to work. The next time an employment program is launched with new and better publicity and "out reach" our friend in the ghetto just does not respond.

The response of the program planners to this phenomenon is illustrated by the Kerner Commission's recommendation that "Special emphasis must be given to motivating the hard-core unemployed." The problem is perplexing. The poor have low self-esteem, lack of drive. We must therefore deal with the "motivational problems" of the poor. In other words, the problem is *them,* not *us.* We do not ask the objective question, "What is wrong?" We ask, "What is wrong *with them*?" The predictable response of a society which, if not racist, responds along remarkably racist lines.

The Commission was certainly not blind to the failing of white society; it recommended special training for supervisory personnel on how to deal with the "hard-core." Well and good, but white racism is not simply an individual characteristic. It is a characteristic of the social structure supported by a huge portion of the population. Most Americans do not see themselves as racists. Thus the personnel manager "impartially" administers an aptitude test which by its nature is biased to the disadvantage of black ghetto dwellers. Or their foreman "impartially" decides that promoting a black to a supervisory position will make white workers hostile and therefore impair plant efficiency, which he is being paid to maximize.

Racism appears to be a very complex phenomenon. Few of us have the confidence to state for certain how deep its roots go or what is required to root it out. It is clear, however, that an important element in the picture is economic competition. It is no accident that the white group most vehemently opposed to having black Americans enjoy equal opportunity in justice are those with the most to lose—the white lower middle class. It is curious, therefore, that until quite recently little attention has been paid to this group, and little analysis made of the impact of poverty programs upon their overt racism.

It is an economic truism that job training and other employment programs do not create jobs. In order for training programs to raise the absolute level of employment (in the short run) there must be, or about to be, vacancies for which qualified personnel are not available and for which training is being given. Under other conditions training merely provides the trainees with the opportunity to become more competitive. The same is true with so-called "job development" programs. Unless jobs are not being filled because of some gross malfunctioning of the employment market, these programs merely give black applicants a *competitive edge* over others. While this may be difficult for some to understand, it is readily perceived by the steel workers and cab drivers of the nation that George Wallace quotes so often.

Whether we operate JOBS (Concentrated Employment Program), or any other purely employment program, the result is to increase the competition among blacks and whites for the same number of jobs in an environment which operates to the disadvantage of the blacks.

All this is occurring in an economic context of shrinking job opportunities for the unskilled and expanding opportunities for the skilled and educated. The greater ease with which black professionals are integrated is commonly attributed to the enlightened attitudes of their white educated colleagues. One wonders, however, how quickly black engineers and economists would be integrated if the job opportunities in these areas were declining.

The point is not that employment programs should not continue, but that we must recognize the great effort and determination it requires on the part of the blacks, and that there is a substantial number of people who do not naturally possess the qualities it takes and therefore cannot succeed in the present system.

To some extent this is recognized in the general conclusion of the Kerner Commission that what is needed are short-run programs to "enrich" the ghetto and long-run programs to integrate the people of the ghetto. (Distinction should be made between enrichment as a goal and enrichment as a stage toward the goal of integration. As the next section will indicate, it is the latter concept with which we are most concerned.) Thus we need programs aimed at restructuring the economic environment of the ghetto to provide a chance for programs emphasizing individual "treatment" to work. In addition to creating the skills necessary to work at a particular occupation, programs will have to create the occupations themselves in an environment free of the pressures of pro-white bias so that the "hard-core" ghetto adult can develop into a confident competitive worker. This means creating an economic foundation within the ghetto itself to provide jobs and opportunities where the people are.

It may mean a great deal more in cost and subsidy (including the provision of protected markets), than that which is being invested in the successful unemployed ghetto resident who finds a permanent job in the suburbs through an employment program, but it must be remembered that we are talking here about those who are not able to compete in that environment and for whom that trip to the suburbs is truly going to another country. For those people it may be that "gilding the ghetto" in the long run is the most effective policy we can have.

SEPARATISM

The charge that economic development of ghetto areas will encourage racial segregation and undo the progress toward integration of the past eight years is a serious one. It must be seriously addressed because, despite some rhetoric to the contrary, a dual society or dual economy is not a realistic solution for anyone, black or white. If ghetto economic development has the effect of encouraging racial segregation, it is not a justifiable program.

We should begin, however, by acknowledging that integration is not merely an interaction between black and white individuals, but a relationship based upon a recognition and respect for the opposite party's equal status. An economic institution such as slavery is clearly not integration (although in the limited sense of personal interaction, the plantation may have been a great deal more integrated than today's typical American metropolitan area). A negotiation between a free buyer and free seller of a product or service clearly is integration. At first glance the employee-employer relationship would seem to qualify. But because the black man's image, both in his own eyes and the eyes of the white, has been one of inferiority, the employee-employer relationship often reinforces this sense of inferiority and makes little headway against a segregated society. If the jobs currently being developed were career jobs which carried with them a sense of worth, one might have some hope that jobs alone could break down the racial barriers dividing our society. But this has not been the case.

ECONOMIC INTEGRATION

What is currently lacking in the black ghetto is the development of institutions which interact with the white community on the basis of equality. The point has been made in many places that such institutions have played an important part in the successful integration of European immigrant groups. Jewish retail stores, Irish police forces, Italian construction companies are the easily recognized examples of this. They all provided a group support for individual contacts with the surrounding dominant ethnic groups. Through this mutual support these institutions developed a power base that forced a respect for their members and at that point real integration became possible.

The function of these institutions is not only to gain respect for the ethnic group involved, but to provide shelter and assistance for the weaker, less competitive individuals. A successful strong business or political machine can afford to carry a few people for the sake of ethnic solidarity. In turn, these institutions can expect the support of their constituencies when they are in competition with institutions controlled by the dominant ethnic groups.

It is clear that this kind of institution-building has been lacking in the black ghetto. The reasons are not difficult to discern, given a knowledge of the unique history of the black man in America. The task now, however, is to help accelerate the building of these institutions by allowing for the development of black economic and political power within the ghetto.

The creation of a black owned business goes far beyond the incremental income that may accrue from ownership of a business. The real significance is its control over resources. The black manager or entrepreneur buys. He hires. He deals with suppliers. He establishes credit. He is engaged in a continual relationship with the white community and by so doing acts as a bridge to the long run goal of a socially and economically integrated society.

It is unlikely that the benefits from this sort of operation can be precisely measured. It involves a process which has implications far beyond the balance sheet of a black owned business. An investment in opening up a menial job for a black man in a white firm, at the most, mildly increases the total level of black-white interaction and hardly has any impact at all on integration. The establishment of a black business, however, increases the amount of real integration in the nation by creating situations in which both parties bargain as equals. Rather than being an obstacle to integration, the growth of black economic power has as a major goal the building of meaningful links between the races, a goal which will not be achieved by exclusive reliance upon employment programs.[1]

COMMUNITY DEVELOPMENT

The events of the past few years have demonstrated how difficult it is to accelerate the pace of residential integration for poor blacks. Even the most optimistic projection of expenditures for public programs aimed at solving this problem implies that a large portion of those currently trapped in urban ghettos will continue to live there for years to come.

[1] For greater elaboration on this point see: Perry, Stewart E. "Black Institutions, Black Separatism, and Ghetto Economic Development," paper read at Society for Applied Anthropology meeting. Mexico City, April 9–15, 1969.

That life must be improved. As part of efforts to improve it, the provision of adequate shopping facilities and consumer services would play an important role. Compared to the typical suburban area, the typical ghetto is woefully underserviced in terms of food and clothing stores, laundry services, banks, etc. Clearly, some of this is attributable to low income, but much of it is a result of the generally deteriorating conditions of life in the ghetto. Threat of riot, refusal of landlords to improve commercial property, impossibly high insurance rates, refusal of suppliers to supply credit and often even to deliver goods to the ghetto merchant, all have drastically reduced the number of businesses serving the inner city. The result in turn is a further drift into hopelessness and an aggravation of the tensions between the ghetto population and the community at large.

Economic development programs aimed at the development of the commercial sector of the ghetto economy will not only increase access to services and quality goods but can help in reducing the higher prices that the poor have to pay to obtain goods. Economic development can provide such things as access to reasonable credit for ghetto businesses, cooperative arrangements to improve merchants' bargaining power with suppliers and financing for decent facilities to attract a greater flow of customers. It can also provide for sufficient competition among ghetto businesses to help assure that reductions in the cost structure are, in turn, passed on to the consumers.

The ultimate goal of community based ghetto economic development should be the total renewal of the ghetto and not only the creation of minor and modest scale ghetto controlled enterprises. This leads us to the issue of ghetto urban renewal programs which, once begun, have either foundered upon the resistance of the ghetto to be renewed, or, *were* never begun due to the obvious hostility of the ghetto to the traditional method utilized in the urban renewal of low-income residential enclaves. Urban renewal of primarily residential ghettos, unlike the development of specific businesses, provides the opportunity for adequate scale investment to radically alter the living environment and, at the same time, create large-scale entrepreneurial opportunities for ghetto controlled community corporations in construction of housing, office buildings, and retail centers, and also in the financing and management of such structures and businesses.

Ghetto controlled urban renewal will also provide the opportunity to exploit new production-construction systems now proven in Europe and Israel and soon to be imported into the United States. This will represent a major opportunity for ghetto entrepreneurs to share in a new technology at the earliest stage of its development.

This may be seen as "separatism" with a vengeance, but it appears to be the only approach available to the government that would be acceptable to current ghetto leadership. It is the only alternative to governmental paralysis in urban renewal. Such an approach may well achieve the stated goals of both urban renewal and black economic development.

LEADERSHIP MODELS

Another social benefit is the establishment of a black entrepreneurial and managerial class within the ghetto itself to provide the leadership and models for male behavior which the ghettos so sorely lack. One of the great failures of poverty programs is the failure to attract the uneducated young adult males upon whose shoulders the destiny of the black ghetto ultimately rests. Aside from paid professional staff, the activists in most of these programs have been the "preachers and the women." Manpower training programs which at the beginning did attract the young males have in too many cases resulted in dead ends. The result is that the models are still not there and we still search in vain for motivation. A principal hypothesis of ghetto enterprise development programs is that they can attract and engage the interest of young males. Business in American society is man's work. It carries with it the independence and power and the promise of reward which no other program can match.

THE BENEFITS OF NEIGHBORHOOD CONTROL

The renewed interest in black enterprise has moved beyond the traditional organizational modes of doing business. Some of these new organizational arrangements, such as those which involve joint ventures between black businessmen and established white firms, protected subcontract markets, and franchises are variations on old themes. In one way or another they continue the basic models of individual entrepreneurship or corporate capitalism. Thus aid is given to existing or potential individual businessmen in an effort to overcome and compensate for the patterns of discrimination they face. In this regard the black businessman is treated like a separate problem group—like the aged, or pre-kindergarten children, or high school dropouts between the ages of 17 and 21.

It is undeniable that minority businessmen are discriminated against. The great exertions a black businessman must go through in order to obtain the considerations other businessmen take for granted have severely restricted the growth of a black middle class. Programs to expand credit availability, to provide technical assistance, to liberalize bonding and insurance standards and to provide easier access to markets for minority enterpreneurs should be immediately intensified. It may be, however, that by limiting our energies to solving the problems of the black businessman we are missing another, somewhat different, opportunity for helping to resolve the urban crisis.

This opportunity reflects the evolution of ghetto poverty programs and ghetto organizations over the past four or five years. While any generalizations about so complex a system as the urban ghetto should be made with great care, many, if not most, of the active leadership groups seem to have gone through roughly parallel experiences. At the beginning, the poverty organizations had a decidedly welfare and social service orientation. The people running programs by and large were those who began from some organizational base—churches and civil rights groups, settlement houses, social service organizations, etc. After a while, however, the increase in resources and power represented by the local community action program and its affiliates began to draw in younger people and, in staff jobs, black male leaders. At the same time, the program orientation changed. Manpower training became the major thrust, which reinforced the development of black male leadership. For the reasons cited in the previous section, manpower programs have been disappointing and the belief in (and thus the importance of) short-term integration on the part of this new leadership has diminished.

We are now, therefore, at a point where a new generation of black male leadership is emerging in the neighborhoods and ghetto organizations. This is a leadership anxious to test its strength and eager to build on the growing black consciousness of its constituency. For many, the next most logical program step is in the area of economic development. Economic development programs not only have the promise of creating employment and income and entrepreneurial experience, but in the eyes of many black leaders, they offer freedom from the white man's charity which they feel is essential for the growth of self-confidence and self-respect among the black population. Since federal programs and federal bureaucrats are the most immediate manifestation of the white man's charity, they are often the first target.

From the local level, federal grant programs appear extremely haphazard, and often sinister. They are uncoordinated (an approach which has certain virtues) and are subject to delays, red tape, and political whimsy. Attempting to increase "administrative efficiency" is not the answer. The trouble is not with the people who run the bureaucratic system but with the system itself. As long as programs are subject to fiscal year funding and as long as the critical decisions are made by individual bureaucrats (no matter how bright or well-intentioned) and thereby subject to political pressures, rational planning and mutual confidence will be hard to come by.

Inasmuch as "independence" is so often equated with "financial independence" in our society, it is quite natural that the recent experience should generate an interest in controlling resources through ownership of business. At times this results in the naive assumption that meaningful social programs could be financed from the immediate profits of black-owned businesses. But short of this, there is much sense in the notion that (aside from whatever income benefits may occur) ownership and control of businesses and other economic institutions provide an independent base for the extension of influence that federal programs cannot provide. It may well be that in the long run an expansion of business ownership by the black community organizations will do more to change the schools, attitudes of policy, etc., than categorical federal grants could ever do. A fundamental change in the milieu of the ghetto may produce such a serendipitous effect.

The fact that community organizations perceive that economic development meets their needs does not by itself justify a public investment in economic development programs. There are, however, at least two important programmatic reasons for establishing economic development programs with broad based community support. First of all, it is becoming increasingly more difficult for any federal program to operate in a ghetto without reference to the social and political forces within the ghetto. The Civil Rights movement and several years of operating community action programs have made a change in the ghetto environment. Poor black people are generally more sophisticated about their plight than used to be the case, and they have become skilled in the techniques of organization and communication with the relevant elements in the white community. As a result, it has become virtually impossible to implement any meaningful program without active community participation. The drive for community control is not a figment of some social scientists' imagination. Regardless of the ultimate fate of the concept, it is an honest alternative generated by the failure of traditional institutions to respond to the legitimate human needs of the ghetto population. The recent history of every new program dealing with inner-city problems testifies to this. Model Cities, in which the demands of inner-city residents all over the country have led to more "citizen participation" than Congress had ever dreamed of, is a case in point. Ghetto economic development must be predicated on these new institutional structures controlled by the ghettoes themselves.

The second program reason for community control is directly related to the fact that the social utility of ghetto economic development involves multiple benefits. As long as programs involve single, separate, quantifiable outputs such as total employment, total number of houses built, etc., a strong case can be made for having the ultimate control of the program in the hands of the technicians who are better equipped to achieve these goals and to optimize the various combinations of benefit-cost relationships. As previously described, however, ghetto economic development involves multiple goals and thus requires that trade-off decisions be made involving non-quantifiable comparisons. Given the fact that the state of the art of cost-benefit analysis is, and for the near term future will continue to be, much too crude to permit any semblance of objective cross comparisons of social benefits, the question becomes, Who should decide between social benefits? If both cost the same, does a program that brings a supermarket to a ghetto area result in more social benefit than an electronics subcontracting plant which hires more men but does not add to the living environment? Is it better to invest a given amount in such a way as to create ten entrepreneurs or thirty unskilled workers? These are questions that will involve subjective and arbitrary judgments. If someone has to make these judgments, it is a reasonable assumption that the perception of the community which has to suffer any mistakes is a better guide than the perception of outside professionals who lack both the conceptual framework and the data for rational analysis. The population of target areas know what it is to live without adequate shopping facilities. They know what it is to live amid an army of unemployed, unskilled males.

This does not mean that ghetto residents can develop their community without outside help. It is as wrong-headed to think that poor unskilled people can operate successful programs alone as it is to assume that professionals can operate programs alone. This is particularly true in programs of business development which by nature involve complex interrelationships between people, considerable technical competence, and presume a certain common frame of reference among participants. The trick, therefore, is to find the combination of community control and technical capability which will produce responsive policies and competent programs. In effect, the authors support the partnership concept between black ghetto institutions and the reigning white establishment, with government playing a "marriage broker" role by equipping the ghetto institutions with the fiscal base to negotiate as equals. Without this governmental role it is unlikely that such "marriages" will be consummated in our time.

From the point of view of public policy, there is a final advantage in community controlled programs. Conventional programs in this area, such as those run by the Small Business Administration and the Economic Development Administration, are built upon an assumption of arbitrary power by the administering bureaucracy. The power to finance one man and deny another lies in most instances with individual bureaucrats whose interests and goals may or may not be in sympathy with the stated goals of a program. More important, perhaps, is that the existence of arbitrary power makes every decision subject to political pressure.

In the private sector, the existence of this kind of power on the part of individuals in financial institutions can be rationalized since, in theory at least, all action can be judged on the basis of maximizing profitability. In the public sector, however, there is no profit guide and political decisions (constrained only by the possibility of large losses) are made much more easily.

The question, therefore, arises as to why individual bureaucrats should have the power to grant public resources to individuals. It would seem that allowing representative community organizations to make the judgments with the aid of competent technical assistance is basically a more legitimate means of disbursing the public treasury.

EVALUATION

Identification of social benefits is just a first step. The probability of a continued shortage of public expenditures on ghetto problems suggests that each and every investment in economic development as well as other programs must be scrutinized closely in order to gain the maximum effectiveness for such expenditures.

If the foregoing description of the multiple benefits of ghetto economic development and the nature of those benefits is valid, it is clear that much broader and more sophisticated evaluation techniques must be developed. The problem is not unique to economic development programs. In fact, the absence of evaluation procedures adequate to deal with multi-goal programs and non-quantifiable benefits may be a critical bottleneck to the development of innovative programs. As long as numbers are the only possible justification for program judgments (other than politics) our ability to resolve our domestic problems will be inhibited, even if available resources expand. The spectacle of federal officials solemnly describing to the Congress the numerical benefits of programs which all objective observers agree have failed, but which continue because they generate quantifiable outputs, is a commentary on the *real* failure of social science.

In developing new evaluation techniques for ghetto business programs, the following principles must be considered:

1. Since the participation in decision-making by the target community is essential in order to arrive at trade-offs, the evaluation of the program must also include the community's own perception of the net effectiveness of a given program or set of programs.
   Random samples of the ghetto population should be made periodically. Questions can be designed to provide information on postulated

benefits of specific programs, e.g., the effect of local black entrepreneurship on the aspirations of young males, the extent to which ownership and control of resources has increased the degree of respect being shown ghetto people by representatives of the community at large.

Questions can also be designed to gather information on degree of total satisfaction with programs, thus implicitly dealing with the effectiveness of trade-offs between goals. All programs involving substantial expenditures should be subject to an ongoing evaluation by the ghetto residents and no major program decisions should be made without an analysis of this kind of data.

2. Both economic development programs and the problems to which they are addressed exist in a relatively long-term framework. The building up of an economic power base in the ghetto as a means of attaining the full integration of society cannot be judged a success or failure in the space of a fiscal year. It is not unusual for successful new businesses to take three years to come into the black, and it will certainly take as long for complex community based programs to begin to show significant measurable final outputs. This does not mean that programs cannot be evaluated at all before several years have elapsed. Incidents in the process of program implementation can be identified and used to measure individual performance. It does mean, however, that short-term payoffs are likely to be rare and if the expectation of such benefits is aroused economic development programs are sure to fail. It would be the height of irresponsibility to establish evaluation requirements which do not allow for a sufficient length of time for economic development programs to work out their impact.
3. Finally, the evaluation of social utility must proceed beyond the analysis of available quantifiable data. If the program goals involve more than employment and income, then they must be evaluated in terms which also include more than employment and income. This requires courage. The attractiveness of conventional statistical data is its ability to serve as a substitute for individual judgment and therefore absorb the blame for program mistakes. In this capacity, it serves Congressmen and bureaucrats (in both public and private sectors) and provides a sound long-term market for highly specialized statistical services. The attempt to go beyond the easily quantifiable must be made, however, for without some understanding of the social benefits of economic development the program will not survive long enough to be effective.
4. Due to the absence of adequate evaluation methods, and recognizing that everything related to programming in the ghetto appears to be charged with an exaggerated rhetoric generating either excessively hopeful expectations or a feeling of being "conned" again, it is the authors' conviction that it is most important that black economic development not be oversold as a panacea. Community based black economic development should be presented as the latest weapon in the fight against poverty and racism, but not meant to supplant or supersede the manpower and social service programs currently extant. In the age of promotion this is an essential caution.

To sum up, the development of black owned enterprises with a strong community base can achieve a number of social benefits that other programs cannot. It may well be that the cost "per achievement" will be higher than the cost "per job" of the conventional approaches of the anti-poverty program. If so, the nation will have to decide whether the social benefits described above, which include those aimed at helping provide a permanent resolution of our social crisis through the creation of strong economic institutions, are worth the cost.

John McClaughry

3

Black Ownership and National Politics

"Richard Nixon's radio speech on the need for the development of black capitalism and ownership in the ghetto could prove to be more constructive than anything yet said by the other Presidential candidates on the crisis of the cities." Thus wrote the New York *Times'* Tom Wicker of the future President's two-part address on "Bridges to Human Dignity," delivered on April 25 and May 2, 1968.

It is perhaps an overstatement to suggest that two speeches of Mr. Nixon's launched the idea which came to be labelled "black capitalism." Yet it cannot be gainsaid that his eloquent exposition of the principles of black ownership did much to accelerate national interest in minority ownership and economic development.

To anyone schooled in the historic Republican philosophy, the "Bridges" speeches represented only a carrying forward of time-honored principles to meet new needs. Yet to those—including many blacks—who held highly critical views of the former Vice President, the speeches produced a certain amount of shock. Here was the conservative nemesis of the Great Society saying that it was time for the establishment to listen to black militants. Here was the apostle of "law and order" saying that the nation needed more black ownership, for from that could flow—black power!

The Nixon philosophy was forthright: "To have human rights,"

JOHN MCCLAUGHRY *is president of McClaughry Associates, Inc. A former special assistant to Richard M. Nixon during the election campaign and transition period of 1968, Mr. McClaughry took part in the development and drafting of the Community Self-Determination Act on behalf of the Congress of Racial Equality while a fellow at the Institute of Politics of the John F. Kennedy School of Government at Harvard University.*

he said, "people need property rights—and never has this been more true than in the case of the Negro today." [He must have] "the economic power that comes from ownership, and the security and independence that come from economic power. More black jobs in white-owned enterprises are still needed," he said, "but it has to be accompanied by an expansion of black ownership, of black capitalism. We need more black employers, more black businesses. . . . We have to get private enterprise into the ghetto. But, at the same time, we have to get the people of the ghetto into private enterprise—as workers, as managers, as owners."

The ideas had been discussed with Nixon by two perceptive confidants, law partner Leonard Garment and speech writer Raymond K. Price, Jr. Nixon listened to their ideas, added some of his own thinking, and worked with them to shape the product for public consumption. But he was deeply apprehensive that his voicing of those ideas would hurt him with conservatives, particularly Southerners, whose votes he needed to win his party's nomination in August, still three months away.

In his Oregon hotel suite, Nixon pondered the question. Then, in a moment of minor drama, he turned to Garment and Price. "I'll get skinned for this in the South," he told them, "but I am going to say it anyway because I am convinced it is right."

For once, the vaunted political judgment of an old pro was in error. The reaction was instantaneous and highly favorable—in some cases verging on pleasant incredulity. *Time* magazine devoted nearly a full page to a verbatim reproduction of his remarks. Conservative papers like the *New York Daily News, Wall Street Journal,* and *Dallas Morning News* applauded. Even Roy Innis, militant leader of CORE, offered the observation that Nixon made more sense on racial matters than anybody else aspiring to the Presidency, making it clear that he included Robert Kennedy.

But, for all its eloquence, "Bridges" left open almost as many questions as it answered—questions on which Nixon was to throw absolutely no light throughout the remainder of his campaign. What did "black capitalism," as the press quickly labelled it, really mean?

It was clear from the Nixon speeches that he had in mind an expansion of black entrepreneurship. This was, however, scarcely revolutionary. Organizations such as the ICBO (Interracial Council for Business Opportunity) and the Negro Industrial and Economic Union (now the Black Economic Union) were already promoting minority business ownership. The Economic Opportunity Loan provisions of the Economic Opportunity Act had already been in operation for over three years. The new Small Business Administrator, Howard Samuels, a New York Democrat, was aggressively moving to implement a major black-oriented small business effort for the Johnson Administration. (He describes some of the results in chapter 5.)

It was clear, too, that Nixon espoused the idea of strengthening black financial institutions. What was not clear was whether "black capitalism" (a term used only twice in the first speech, and not at all in the second) embraced consumer ownership—as in cooperative retail establishments. Nor was it clear whether agricultural producing and marketing co-ops came within his meaning. Perhaps most crucially, it was not clear whether Nixon conceived of any kind of black ownership which extended broadly across the ghetto and to major profit-making industries, or whether he advocated merely the skimming off of the most talented ghetto dwellers to make them into "Mom and Pop" store owners.

Nixon's unwillingness to attempt any further refinement and exposition of the principles enunciated inspired widely varying interpretations of "black capitalism." Those who saw in it their own view of what should be done praised Nixon; those who saw it in some other view attacked him.

The immediate tangible product of the Nixon speeches was a two-hour meeting with the leaders of the Congress of Racial Equality (CORE), Roy Innis and Floyd McKissick, in Nixon's Fifth Avenue apartment in May 1968. The CORE leaders had for several months been working with their own experts, black and white, to develop a plan for dramatically broadened black ownership of businesses and control over community service programs; thus their keen interest in the sentiments of the future President.

Curiously, politics was not even discussed. Nixon sought the views of the black leaders; Innis and McKissick came to verify the depth of his commitment to the philosophy expressed in his "Bridges" speeches. As Nixon spoke, they became convinced of his philosophical commitment. But they also wanted his help—help in recruiting additional top-flight volunteer technicians to help them construct major national legislation to make possible the program they had outlined, and in securing Republican support for the legislation in Congress. In those quests, they were successful.

As CORE completed work on the legislation, it also developed an unprecedented political strategy. It called for temporarily ignoring liberal Democrats in Congress and concentrating first on Republicans and conservatives. If they could be sold a product, CORE reasoned, liberal support could be obtained with little difficulty later. Since blacks had always directed their pleas to the liberals, usually in Democratic ranks, this conscious choice to pursue Republicans and conservatives was an historic first.

The product was another matter. For months, Innis and McKissick had been developing the ideas of black-owned community corporations, which would own productive businesses and channel the profits into services needed in the black community. This, they reasoned, would provide an independent source of income—revenues not extracted from the white power structure, but earned by black capital and black labor and controlled by black people themselves. Now, work on what became the Community Self-Determination Act accelerated rapidly.

First there were more brainstorm sessions, held at the Institute of Politics at Harvard's John F. Kennedy School of Government. The sessions were intriguing for their composition as well as for the ideas considered. There were Harvard Law professors and graduate students from the business school. One expert corporate tax attorney flew in twice from Chicago. Even as Nixon staff members and law associates moved in and out, Humphrey and Kennedy staff members were consulted and kept informed. Bearded militants from Harlem and soft-spoken blacks from the deep South sat side by side with radical economists and Republican businessmen. Finally, astonishingly, a consensus began to emerge.

By the eighth draft, the plan was complete in its essentials. The basic concept was a broadly owned community development corporation based in an area defined by the people themselves through a complicated referendum process. The corporation would own a family of businesses, which might range from a shoe shine stand to a major factory and which would be located both inside and outside the community area. With the profits from these enterprises, the community corporation would finance community service projects of the people's own choice, such as day-care centers, basic education, legal aid, non-profit housing, health care and the like.

To finance the acquisitions of the community corporation, the bill authorized the creation of community development banks and a national secondary financing institution, a system resembling a large part of the present Farm Credit System. The community corporation would also have access to funds to enable it to hire the managerial and technical expertise, the lack of which was admittedly the most serious bottleneck to rapid progress.

The tax provisions of the Act were all important. One group of tax amendments defined a unique status for community development corporations. In essence, community corporations and their subsidiaries would pay little or no taxes. The tax-augmented profit flow would be applied only to community services and not used to line private pockets.

The second group of tax amendments encouraged a "turnkey" relationship between a community corporation and a major company like General Electric or Xerox. Under these provisions, the outside—and presumably white-owned—company would enter into a "turnkey" agreement to create an operating factory, store, or other facility; train local people to become its managers and employees; and then sell the economically viable facility to the community corporation. This was considered the heart of the economic argument for the bill. Without the turnkey provisions, poor community corporations could scarcely be expected to operate competitive, profit-making businesses; if there were no profit flow, there would be no community services; and with no community services, the incentive for broad participation in affairs of the community would be markedly reduced.

By July, the draftsmen had completed their work and action shifted to Washington. Four key GOP Congressmen were approached for sponsorship in the House. Rep. (now Senator) Charles Goodell of New York was chairman of the Research and Planning Committee of the House Republican Conference and had long been the party's leading spokesman on poverty matters. Rep. Thomas B. Curtis of Missouri was a most creative and influential member of the Ways and Means Committee. Rep. William B. Widnall of New Jersey was the ranking member of the Banking and Currency Committee. And Rep. Bob Taft, Jr. of Ohio had chaired the Republican Coordinating Committee Task Force that had produced a major GOP statement on "New Directions for Urban America."

Readers of the Washington *Post* of July 12, 1968, were startled to learn of the sponsorship of the CORE bill by these four Republican worthies, who appeared in a page one photograph with three bearded Harlem militants, led by Roy Innis. Some 36 Republican Congressmen eventually sponsored the measure. Much later, they were joined by a smaller group of Democrats, including the House's most militant black spokesman, Rep. John Conyers of Michigan.

In the Senate, a curiously diverse group of 26 Senators, evenly divided between the parties, united to introduce the Act a week later. It featured liberals from Sen. Gaylord Nelson, Wisconsin Democrat, Sen. George McGovern, South Dakota Democrat and Oklahoma's Sen. Fred Harris, now chairman of the Democratic National Committee, through liberal Republicans like Illinois' Charles Percy and New York's Jacob Javits, all the way to Southern Republicans like Sen. Howard Baker of Tennessee and even Sen. John Tower of Texas. In the background, Vice President Humphrey urged his Senatorial lieutenants to lend their support. Nixon issued a statement urging prompt consideration of the bill, while avoiding an outright endorsement. Only Eugene McCarthy and Nelson Rockefeller kept a cautious distance from the action. (McCarthy, however, endorsed the principles in a major address shortly thereafter.)

No one expected any kind of Congressional action on a 180-page bill introduced just before the national party conventions in a presidential year. Although the concepts of the bill were in large measure referred to with approval in both party platforms, the legislation itself did not become an issue in the remaining campaign. The bill did, however, raise so many fundamental questions about black-white relations, economic philosophies, the federal anti-poverty programs and beliefs, and numerous related matters that it quickly became the center of attention among those most concerned with developments in this area.

The most important of the questions raised, around which bitter controversy swirled, were these:

Ownership vs. Jobs

The premise of the bill was that ownership and control of productive wealth and consumer goods (such as housing) were at least as important as the mere provision of jobs alone. CORE, for example, condemned any tax incentive scheme based on continued white ownership of job-producing facilities. To them, a big white company's decision to locate a job-producing facility in a ghetto was less a conscientious effort to reduce urban problems than one more lightly disguised form of economic colonialism of the black ghetto. Opponents argued that ownership was far less important than men on payrolls, and that the unemployed black man most of all needed a decent paying job to begin his climb to economic security.

Monolith vs. Diversity

The bill postulated an all-embracing community corporation which, after a lengthy certification process, would hold exclusive sway in a geographical area. Proponents saw this as an essential feature if the black community was to acquire any unity and power. Others, however, were concerned that the community corporations, though without the power to compel participation, issue regulations, or levy taxes, would become local despotisms. Despite some provisions in the bill designed to mitigate this problem, opponents argued that it would kill freedom of choice and diversity. If only one community corporation could be created in a given area, they reasoned, every "street baron" would struggle to control the corporation and through it take advantage of his helpless rivals.

Isolation vs. Integration

Since the bill sprang from CORE, a black organization advocating a strongly separatist philosophy, liberal integrationists saw the bill as a device for perpetuating segregation of the races. The presence of certain conservative sponsors of the legislation in Congress did little to allay their fears. The bill itself was ambiguous on this point. Some provisions hinted at an entirely ghetto-oriented activity; others suggested economic penetration of the larger economy and substantial economic activity outside the community area proper—particularly when ghetto economic conditions argued against any attempt to locate facilities there. Backers of the bill argued that immediate efforts to force assimilation of blacks into the larger society could have little immediate impact, since the great bulk of urban blacks would continue to live in the ghettoes for a number of years anyway. Thus, they reasoned, the effort should be directed toward building black power and black control where blacks are now. Those who wanted to move to the suburbs should be free to do so. But such emigration, they reasoned, would do little to solve the problems of those left behind and—by a brain drain effect—would probably reduce the opportunities for broad progress.

Fragmentation vs. Order

Proponents of the bill saw as one of the major problems of ghetto life the inability of people to surmount the fragmentation and disunity so characteristic of their social environment—a fragmentation not infrequently the result of well-meaning governmental efforts that failed. To proponents, then, the community corporation idea held merit as a unifying mechanism. The prospect of effective community control of revenues from business operations and the dispensation of needed services, they suggested, would produce incentives to widespread participation in a common cause. This in turn would lead to a reduction of the alienation and lack of motivation so endemic in poor communities. Opponents, however, charged that the organizational process—involving elaborate pledge card and referendum procedures to preserve openness and free choice—would result not in new order and stability, but in internecine political warfare between rival factions seeking community dominance.

Democratic Participation vs. Competence

An explicit goal of the community corporation was the widespread participation of the poor in shaping their own destinies. At the same time, the success of the corporation hinged upon effective management, both of business subsidiaries and of the community corporation itself. Opponents of the bill argued that in broadening the decision-making base in a poor community, any semblance of competence in the business sense, at the very least, would become highly unlikely. Voluminous experience with the community action programs of the federal War on Poverty supported this view. Proponents, however, argued that poor people were quite competent to decide how best to *spend* the available funds to meet their community's needs. As for *raising* the funds through business operations, the proponents pointed out that under the bill the businesses would be managed by a semi-independent Business Management Board, relatively immune to popular passions.

Equal vs. Preferential Treatment

Even proponents of the bill were divided on whether the community corporation should dispense benefits and services only to its shareholders, or to the population of the area at large. As a result, the bill left this important question to local option. The corporation could either make its services available to the entire community, including non-shareholders; or it could function as a sort of neighborhood "key club" whose benefits only shareholders could enjoy.

Personal Profits vs. Collective Benefits

A particularly sharp controversy quickly emerged over the use of the business profits. Some proponents of the bill argued strongly that the profits (after taxes and reinvestment) of the corporation and its subsidiaries should be plowed into community services rather than paid out as dividends to individuals. Congress, they said, would never authorize the purely nominal taxation called for in the bill if the resulting profits were channeled into private pockets. Further, the aggregate amount of profits could have an important effect on the welfare and motivation of the whole community, but the small amounts available to each individual through distribution would be virtually meaningless. Finally, if the community wanted to distribute to individual shareholders, it could do so merely by waiving the favorable tax treatment and accepting normal corporate taxation. Critics, however, attacked very sharply the idea of collectivizing the profits for community services. This, they said, was a travesty of free enterprise; it was, in fact, neighborhood communism. More practically, they argued that the lack of personal profit would make the whole enterprise highly unattractive, especially so for the talented individuals most needed for managerial and leadership roles.

Substitute vs. Supplement

Particularly strong criticism came from those who viewed the Community Self-Determination Act as a spurious substitute for Great Society social legislation. Citing the statements of some conservative sponsors that the bill was intended to replace present antipoverty legislation, the liberal-labor-civil rights-foundation group attacked the Act as another conservative device to permit the strangulation of their own favorite social programs. Then, they argued, when the self-determination idea fails in practice, there will be nothing, leaving the nation back where it was a decade ago. In short, they envisioned the destruction of all they had fought to create over opposition of many of the people who looked upon the self-determination act as a promising new idea. Most proponents countered by observing that basic public responsibilities in education, health, and the like would continue, act or no act; and that the community corporations would become the logical vehicles for implementation of a number of present programs.

Utopia vs. Reality

The act was also attacked as hopelessly faulty in its economic premises. Even under incredibly favorable conditions, it was argued, community corporations could not come close to paying for the services needed by the community. There was simply not enough profit to be made in a ghetto or depressed rural area. Proponents countered by observing that the bill did not limit the economic activity to the ghetto or rural area; that even modest income could be vitally important as seed money or matching portions; and that in any case a federal profit-matching grant could be used to multiply the value of the community's self-help efforts. In the absence of hard data to permit a responsible assessment of the economic model, this debate tended to produce more noise than enlightenment.

The CDC vs. the Entrepreneur

In addition to creating a capital financing device for community corporation enterprises, the bill also sought to make the community development bank an added source of business capital for local entrepreneurs and corporations. Despite these good intentions, critics raised two important objections. First, they said, the community development bank will always give preference to loan applications from the community corporation, since the bank is itself owned by the community corporation. Only if there is unused capital will the bank consider a loan to an independent entrepreneur; hence the bank is not likely to expand his access to business financing at all. Second, they saw the whole community corporation structure as a subtle effort to expropriate independent business in the community. They pointed out that the system envisioned would permit the community corporation to establish subsidiaries in direct competition with entrepreneurs. The subsidiaries, with greater access to funds and resources available to them through the provisions of the bill, would drive the little guy out of business.

Proponents agreed that the community development bank would give preference to loan applications from its parent community corporation. But, they said, it was important to remember that there was no government subsidy involved. While the new bank would probably be much more sympathetic than pre-existing financial institutions, it would still have to charge a market interest rate to retain its solvency. In addition, there were safeguards against a community corporation subsidiary undercutting competing entrepreneurs. It could not engage in unfair trade practices, such as selling below cost to attract the competitor's business, without running afoul of the Federal Trade Commission. Further, operating on a little or no-profit basis would mean no funds for community services. Thus a clamor could be expected from shareholders who wanted profits for day care centers, basic education programs, vest pocket parks, etc. Permitting the United States Community Development Bank to make loans directly to entrepreneurs in community corporation areas was suggested as one means of reducing any problem that might arise.

With issues as fundamental and far-reaching as these, it was not hard to understand why the Community Self-Determination Act provoked such a torrent of controversy.

With President Nixon's inauguration, attention focused on the efforts his administration might make to push forward in this area. His Assistant for Urban Affairs, Dr. Daniel P. Moynihan, was known to believe that employment was the all-important question for minority citizens, and should take preference over broad-based community economic efforts. Dr. Arthur Burns, Counselor to the President in charge of domestic program development, seemed to believe in the use of tax incentives for economic development of disadvantaged urban and rural areas, but gave no indication of interest in finding ways to implement the minority ownership theme set forth in the Nixon speeches of 1968. On the other hand, Secretary George Romney of the Department of Housing and Urban Development had expressed considerable interest in the ownership theme, dating back to his profit-sharing plans at American Motors in the Fifties, and continuing throughout his relations with the black community while Governor of Michigan. James Farmer, the newly named Assistant Secretary of

Health, Education and Welfare and the Administration's most prominent black official, was wholly behind the Self-Determination Act, and had been present with his former CORE colleagues when the Senate version was introduced in 1968.

By March of 1969 it became apparent that Commerce Secretary Maurice Stans would play a key role in guiding Administration efforts in this area. By Executive Order in March, President Nixon gave Stans a broad mandate to coordinate a host of federal agencies and programs through a new Office of Minority Business Enterprise, headed by an assistant to the Secretary of Commerce. The new office, however, was given no program funds of its own, nor was it given authority to control funds budgeted to other agencies. Its task seemed to be to persuade participating agencies to cooperate in a series of showcase projects. Skeptics were quick to note that similar efforts to persuade without controlling had proven considerably less than successful in the past.

Stans was also close-mouthed about his own concept of "minority business enterprise," the successor slogan to the unfortunate term "black capitalism." No one doubted that Stans was enthusiastic about the "Andrew Carnegie model" for minority economic development—start with a dime, borrow a dollar, rise early and work late, and build yourself a steel mill. The question was whether Stans had any broader concept of minority business enterprise. Would his new office seek to promote retail cooperatives? New financial institutions? Rural production and marketing cooperatives? Profit-sharing and stock option plans? Minority ownership of a piece of major national corporations? Broadly-based community development corporations? In response to a direct question at his news conference announcing the establishment of the office, the Commerce Secretary stated, somewhat uncertainly, that cooperative and community corporation ventures would fall within the office's purview; but the apparent newness of these concepts to the Secretary caused some apprehension among proponents of the Community Self-Determination Act and related measures. In his new assistant and his deputies, however, Stans has personnel of unquestioned sympathy for a broadly conceived effort.

The fate of the Community Self-Determination Act itself was unclear. Like any piece of legislation that attacked current concepts and advanced fundamentally different approaches, the act bore the weight of heavy criticism. But the old programs, as even the liberal critics were sullenly conceding, had largely failed. The time was clearly ripe for major new departures. That fact was keenly recognized even by those who were yet uncertain about the most desirable direction.

The most important figure is clearly the President of the United States. How well Richard Nixon understands the problems and opportunities, whose counsel he most readily receives, in what direction he chooses to move, at what pace he proceeds, whether he seizes the initiative or merely responds to the urgings or attacks of others—all these factors will bear heavily on the coming struggle to bring increased equity, power, and order to the excluded minorities of America.

Roy Innis

4

Separatist Economics: A New Social Contract

There exists today a crisis of immense proportions within the boundaries of the United States of America. This crisis is the direct result of the breakdown of the relationship between black and white people in our society. It was scarcely a good relationship to begin with. For blacks it has been degrading and dehumanizing; for whites, it has been abrasive, guilt-ridden, and a perpetual thorn. Over the decades, the problem has festered and spread to the point where it now threatens to destroy the entire political organism in which it is rooted.

Even at this late date, we can provide an alternative to the collision course of whites and blacks in this country. But to do so, we must develop entirely new solutions to the massive problems of the past. The present programs and plans offered by well-meaning agencies, groups, and individuals are entirely insufficient. Aside from the fundamental lack of understanding in the past of the nature and degree of racism in this country, there has been a failure to coordinate the multiplicity of suggested "solutions." Such solutions, in any case, have never been structured by black people. They have always been structured by whites who interpreted our needs and in many cases designed these solutions to accommodate their own needs.

Where the collision of black and white is concerned, we have falsely assumed in America that a contract or constitution designed for a dominant majority, with distinct attributes, self-interests, and needs, could simply be adapted, by minor modifications, to fit the needs of

---

ROY INNIS *is national director of CORE (Congress of Racial Equality) and co-publisher of the* Manhattan Tribune.

a significant minority with different attributes, interests, and needs. Obviously, this has not worked. A crucial weakness has been the lack of control by black people over the institutions that surround them: institutions that not only establish imposed values for them but also control the flow of goods and services within their communities, thereby shaping the quality of their lives. The black community sees these institutions in the hands of people with interests too often at odds with their own. Thus, schools in black neighborhoods too often do not teach, sanitation departments do not protect, employment departments do not find jobs, welfare departments do not give adequate relief, housing departments do not give decent housing. Most ironic of all, human rights departments do not guarantee human rights.

The obvious solution, then, is a *new social contract,* to be drawn in the mutual interest of both parties. This contract must redefine the relationship between blacks and whites, to the extent that black people are recognized as a major interest group. While this redefinition is in progress, there are palpable changes to be implemented.

Large, densely populated black areas, especially in urban centers, must have a change in status. They must become political sub-divisions of the state, instead of sub-colonial appendages of the cities. Blacks must manage and control the institutions that service their areas, as has always been the case for other interest groups. There is an immediate need in the institutions of education, health, social service, sanitation, housing, protection, etc. Black people must be able to control basic societal instruments in the social, political, and economic arenas.

DEFINITIONS

In short, black people must seek liberation from the dominance and control of white society. Nothing less than this liberation will allow black people to determine their own destinies.

Perhaps, at this point, a few definitions are in order. There is always a controversy as to whether our tactics, our objectives, are reformist or revolutionary. In my own view, black people at this state of their development are not and should not be talking about some romantic thing called revolution, but rather a more pragmatic and necessary step called liberation. There is a difference between the two. A revolution, of course, occurs where one class of a national group rebels against another class of that same group, as in the Russia of 1917, the France of the late 18th Century. Liberation come about in a setting of two distinct groups, where one is suppressing the other. Jews caught in Egypt in the time of the Pharaohs did not talk about revolution against what was the most powerful and formidable military machine of the time. They talked about liberation—separating themselves from Egyptians.

We black nationalists, too, must speak of separating ourselves. We live in a setting where one group—not our own—controls the institutions, and the flow of goods and services. We can change our condition by liberating ourselves and placing these vital instruments of social and economic destiny in our own hands. This is what we mean by separation—quite a different matter from segregation, which is the condition that now exists, in fact, throughout the United States.

Separation is a more equitable way of organizing the society. The important distinction is that in such a society the control of goods and services flowing through a distinct geographical area inhabited by a distinct population group would be in the hands of those indigenous to the area. In other words, if we have a clearly defined sociological unit called Harlem, New York City, the people of Harlem will control the flow of goods and services there. The same would hold true for the white areas of New York City: the whites would control their own "action."

In the struggle toward self-determination, there has been a great deal of argument about the order of steps to be taken. Should we be talking first about politics, about culture, or should we be talking about economics? Let me suggest that we can resolve this dilemma by understanding first of all that these three stages of liberation are virtually inseparable. There must be some sort of socio-cultural renaissance if there is to be movement in any other direction. There must be some sort of politico-economic development if the cultural movement is to have any base on which to acquire significance.

My feeling is that we have already begun part of this movement. That is, black people have begun revitalizing their culture, recreating their values. We must now phase in the element of economic growth. The failure of many of the past economic measures—community action, training and hiring programs, and the like—is that they have been little more than board games, depending on some sort of arithmetic progression. What we need to do now is to find the geometric factor that can speed up this process. And that is why we turn to the control of institutions. But some further definition is needed.

CAPITALISM OR DEVELOPMENT

In the new focus on economic control, there has been much talk about something called "black capitalism." Many of our people have been deluded into endless debates centered around this term. There is no such animal. Capitalism, like socialism, is an economic and political philosophy that describes the experience of Europeans and their descendants—Americans. Blacks must innovate, must create a new ideology. It may include elements of capitalism, elements of socialism, or elements of neither: that is immaterial. What matters is that it will be created to fit our needs.

So then black people are not talking about black capitalism. Black people are talking about economic development. We are talking about the creation and the acquisition of capital instruments by means of which we can maximize our economic interests. We do not particularly try to define styles of ownership; we say that we are willing to operate pragmatically and let the style of ownership fit the style of the area or its inhabitants.

The question of autonomy is critical. Any reliable sociological analysis will indicate that we live in natural units called communities. Where whites are concerned, these natural sociological units then become natural political units—political subdivisions of county, state, or federal government. This does not happen with black communities, so that extensive areas like Harlem in New York, Roxbury in Boston, Watts in Los Angeles, exist as colonial appendages of the urban center. In fact, government programs almost always deal with us as part of urban centers, and in terms of the overall condition of those centers. This is something we must resist strenuously, for there is a fundamental conflict of interest between our communities—the so-called ghettos—and the urban centers in which they are situated. The urban centers are managed by political and institutional barons who include our piece of "turf" in their domain. And we see that whenever we make any attempt to change that relationship—political, social, or economic—we meet the massive resistance of these barons. This sort of frustration has led and will continue to lead to disastrous confrontations between blacks and whites.

We understand also that the urban setting, throughout history, has been the energizer of mankind, thus the cradle of change. It is there that blacks, too, will have to find their solutions. We cannot go off to conduct a masquerade of change in newly created little rural centers. But if we are to develop in the urban centers, our position must be newly understood.

There is a very striking similarity between the so-called underdeveloped countries and our underdeveloped black communities. Both have always been oppressed; almost always there is an unfavorable balance of trade with the oppressors or exploiters; both suffer from high unemployment, low income, scarce capital, and we can point to a series of other similarities. But let me point to at least one vital difference. In every so-called underdeveloped country, the people have a measure of sovereignty. They have a vastly greater amount of autonomy compared with the black communities across this country. It seems to me, then, that a natural impetus for our communities is to move to gain that missing ingredient—sovereignty, or at least a greater degree of autonomy and self-determination.

In other words, I am saying there is no way we can divorce economic development from political imperatives. You cannot have economic development unless you have certain supportive political realities, one of which is some degree of self-determination.

THE DIVIDENDS

What economic gratuities would flow from self-determination? Let us consider the massive budgets provided to pay for the goods and services of a single black community (which are then almost always poorly distributed in that community). Take the schools, for example. In a community like Harlem, close to a hundred million dollars is spent yearly for goods and services to supply the schools. We must assume, in fact we know, that in almost every instance those goods and services are purchased from sources outside the community. Now we in the black community pay taxes that are intended to be used to pay for these commodities, so that nominally, all tax monies are returned to us in this form. But what really happens is that our tax monies are returned to agents of the urban centers—the mayor and his commissioners and department heads—who will then use that money to enhance the economic interest of the white-dominated urban center by buying goods and services outside the black communities they are meant to serve.

That same hundred million dollars could have gone, let us say, to a corporation in Harlem put together by two or three black entrepreneurs and awarded a contract to supply books for the Harlem schools. It is immaterial that this hypothetical corporation does not own a publishing house or a printing plant. Neither do the white corporations that presently supply books to the public school system in Cleveland, or New York, or any place else across this country. They are merely middlemen. They buy from someone else and sell to the schools. They move paper from one side of their desk to the other and turn a handsome profit. That kind of profit could be turned just as easily within the black community, to increase its income by the millions. Multiply the massive budgets for the schools by the massive budgets in health and hospital services, sanitation, and all the other urban services, and you get a massive amount of money that represents a guaranteed market.

The name of this in economics is guaranteed market. That is what you have when you are selling to your own institutions: there will always be a demand for your goods and services. If you have control of these institutions you are able to determine who will get the contracts, and you can direct them back to your own people.

So here we see at least one route by which the black people can get a running start in economic development without huge investments in machinery, materials, technical expertise, and without most of the other impediments that are immediately cited when we talk about economic development. And it is a way in which we could secure a maximum return to our community from those precious tax dollars that we pay year after year.

Of course, this same division of interest and diversion of profit has social as well as economic consequences. We must control our schools if we are to upgrade education and pass on positive values to our children. We must control health facilities if we are to cut down our mortality rate. We must control the law enforcement in our areas if the police are to serve their proper function—which is protection, not oppression. In short, we must control every single institution that takes our tax moneys and is supposed to distribute goods and services equitably for us.

Vehicles for Self-Determination

The Congress of Racial Equality has been working to develop vehicles and instruments for black self-determination at both the local and national levels.

THE HARLEM COMMONWEALTH COUNCIL

The first group in America to formalize the advance of black business beyond the "Mom-and-Pop" stage was the Harlem Commonwealth Council in New York. With a controversial grant from the Demonstration Office of the Office of Economic Opportunity, the HCC was organized as a non-profit, tax exempt corporation which invests in profit-making businesses and uses the accumulated income to re-invest in other businesses. The National Association of Manufacturers and McKinsey and Company agreed to provide help, along with two universities.

The HCC's first brochure notes that Harlem's half million people can spend half a billion dollars for consumer goods every year—a sum larger than the gross national product of many underdeveloped nations. Yet, says the brochure, "the economic sickness of Harlem" is that most of this capital is siphoned off from the community by the outsiders who own 80 per cent of Harlem's business volume. "One root problem of Harlem is that almost no one who lives there owns anything."

Accordingly, the goal of HCC is to "bring back to Harlem that internal economic vitality which is essential to social development . . . . It is not enough to attract white-owned industry. Finding jobs for blacks is not enough either, critical as that is. Both of these become enough only if we can also develop Harlem's capital."

To implement its plans, HCC set up a community-based Board of Directors who, with help from the outside consultants, quickly developed their own ability to pick and choose among business opportunities. As objectives they selected those businesses which would meet community needs (e.g., a 24-hour pharmacy selling prescription medicines by their generic names, thus permitting prices considerably lower than those for brand name medicines), and modern businesses which capitalize on Harlem's strategic location in Manhattan (e.g., an Automotive Diagnostic Center near the Triborough Bridge which feeds in traffic from two other boroughs).

The HCC is not looking for yesterday's businesses but tomorrow's opportunities. They are utilizing the most modern market instruments to determine markets and potentials; helping locate business opportunities in Harlem and then finding the potential businessmen to run them; designing training and apprenticeship programs to prepare a black man to run his own business; and providing the technical services to train managers.

THE CLEVELAND PLAN

In Cleveland, Ohio, CORE has projected the development of a consortium of black economic institutions designed to significantly broaden the base of ownership by the black community of productive capital instruments. The Cleveland program is seeking $10 million of funding for a two-year operational budget, to establish sustaining economic institutions through which black residents could be both owners of capital instruments and wage earners. An excerpt from the formal summary of the proposal [1] states this general concept:

> CORENCO (CORE Enterprises Corporation) contends that the way to correct (the economic imbalance between black and white communities) is to effect institutional changes which increase the productive power of under-productive households and individuals so that they may legitimately receive enough income to satisfy their reasonable needs and desires. Although it is a method which would tend to protect existing private property, it would also tend to build a "New Black Economy" in the black community, so financed that it becomes owned in moderately-sized holdings by the great majority of households and individuals who own no productive capital in the existing economy. . . .
>
> New financing techniques can enable the man without capital to buy it, and to pay for it out of the wealth it produces, and therefore to enjoy a new stream of income, if there is a demand for his employment

[1] A copy of this proposal can be obtained from the Congress of Racial Equality, 200 West 135th Street, New York, New York 10030.

—and the only full employment possible in our advanced industrial economy must result from the building and operation of a second economy producing humanly useful and desirable goods—he will then have two sources of income with which, on the one hand, to erase his poverty and, on the other hand, to provide the market—the effective market—for the expanded output by industry and business.

CORENCO will establish research and development teams to promote a wide range of economic projects aimed at creating a black economic infrastructure and increasing black ownership and employment in the institutions that purchase and distribute goods and services in the black community.

THE FEDERAL BILL

Most of the problems we have discussed in this chapter we have tried to deal with, to some degree, in the Community Self-Determination Bill. This bill, created by CORE with a wide spectrum of expert assistance, was introduced before the Congress of the United States in July of 1968, receiving support from all political corners. (Ironically, but not surprisingly, most of the opposition came from labor, from the leadership of the AFL-CIO, which used to proclaim itself the great friend of the black man. In the current history of the civil rights movement and the black power movement, we have had to fight our biggest and toughest battles against the labor unions. More recently, the AFL-CIO has declared itself opposed to so-called black capitalism and thus, by implication, to black self-determination. Meanwhile, of course, they continue to endorse programs advocating jobs for blacks—jobs that the unions themselves consistently prevent us from getting.)

The Community Self-Determination Bill can serve as a social, political, and economic tool by means of which the black communities can make giant strides. Through it, we can create community instruments that can in themselves create community industries; these in turn would produce jobs for men. It would provide for a variety of types of ownership, for community boards in black areas to coordinate economic development and the control of indigenous institutions.

These community boards would be the sole agencies in the black community responsible for both social welfare and economic development. They would give contracts to community industries and raise sound financing for them with the help of a new banking system—community development banks.

As projected, the program will provide incentive for broad-based community ownership. It will contain provisions for research, development, and training, for the development of innovations in health, welfare, education, and other community services. It will provide performance bond guarantees to enable existing industries that cannot now meet bonding requirements to compete for a fair share of contracts for the black communities. It contemplates providing incentives for outside industry to come into our areas—though not to stay. Unlike other programs, we do not want to bring white industries into the black community to create jobs. We want industries to come into the community to create *instruments,* to sell them to us, and then move out.

Will It Work?

So what we are talking about, in the final analysis, is not jobs, but instruments that create jobs. We are not talking about bringing white businesses into black communities, but about building economic instruments that themselves can hire blacks. Nor are we talking merely, as some people seem to construe it, of substituting black ownership of a pants-pressing business for white ownership of a pants-pressing business, for that is looking at the economics of the community on the lowest scale. We are talking about the acquisition of capital instruments on a major scale, to maximize the flow of money in the community and begin that geometric progression toward economic well-being.

This separatist economics, as I choose to call it, is not essentially different from the basic principles of developmental economics employed by any people—for example, the Americans of post-Revolutionary period. It is the manipulation of the economy of black areas in a preferential way to obtain an edge and protect the interests of the community; to place a membrane around the community that allows full commercial intercourse with outside business interests while setting pre-conditions and guidelines advantageous to the community for those who may seek to operate within the community. This principle is known by many names, one of the more familiar being *tariff*.

Will whites go along with this? I must be honest—I do not have an unshakable faith in white people; I have no experience that would support such a faith.

But the underlying assumption of all I have said here is that whites who have the most power (real power) and the most to lose from chaos *will* go along with it; that the Community Self-Determination Bill will become the high-powered vehicle of the new black economy. What I assume is that an enlightened self-interest will head off the impending collision in this country—and I am talking about the enlightened self-interest of black people and white.

For we are past the stage where we can talk seriously of whites acting toward blacks out of moral imperatives. That does not work. Yet we can still talk of change coming about through enlightened self-interest, the prime motivator of orderly change in society throughout the history of mankind. That is the only thing that works without destroying what it seeks to save.

Howard J. Samuels

5

Compensatory Capitalism

The indigenous ghetto resident is born and lives in a state of deprivation—yet he commutes every day into American affluence, to his neo-colonial manufacturing or domestic service job. He moves back and forth daily from sophisticated metropolitan property to his slum. And in doing so, he exports the ghetto's only asset, labor, for unlike frontiers, colonies, or underdeveloped nations, the ghetto has no natural resources to attract foreign capital investment.

What the ghetto black lacks is an effective way into the system with more impact than job training or education. He needs a way to develop himself and his community based on competitive economic achievement. He must have a business stake in the American business culture. There is great hope of this in the "black power" and "black capitalism" movements.

In the most basic sense "black power" means the development of an underdeveloped people to perform and achieve. The business community interest and sympathy for black capitalism is not based on "black power's" alleged perpetuation of segregation. Black and other minority capital accumulation, investment, and development, need not perpetuate segregation. They provide, in fact, an excellent basis for eliminating it and achieving parity. Businessmen are attracted to "black power" because they know it is only on the basis of their own

---

HOWARD J. SAMUELS *is former administrator of the Small Business Administration. A former Under Secretary of Commerce, Mr. Samuels served as chairman of the Citizen's Committee for an Effective Constitution and led the campaign to convene the New York State Constitutional Convention in 1967. Mr. Samuels founded the Kordite Corporation in 1946, and presently serves as a member of a variety of civic and educational groups.*

capability to deliver a product or service in the market place that their businesses can profit. This is what business power initially consists of.

Businessmen and bankers, in addition, control the investment decision—where to put their net profit. The businessman and the banker also know where to get more capital or credit to invest other people's capital. And through participation on welfare boards and community service agencies moreover, businessmen (and others) decide how what everybody gives toward the public welfare is spent. Economic power based on business success is recognized as a legitimate way to social and political power. This is precisely what the black leader wants for himself and his community.

A stake in the system and a say as to how the common wealth is invested are two essential requirements of Jeffersonian democracy. Black capitalism producing this kind of black power is thus thoroughly authentic economic and political leadership, not just a vote and a dole.

Unless our institutions deliver on the basis of these fundamental principles and requirements of the ghetto, we will fail 15 per cent of our population. America as we know it cannot afford, nor perhaps survive, a failure of such magnitude.

Today we measure our progress by the Gross National Product (GNP) and it is frequently remarked that this is only a quantitative measure not a qualitative one. One of the qualitative measures by which we should be judged and which may be the best test of our society, is how much access to a stake in the system we provide to minorities who are not yet a part of it.

It will be a test both of actions and policies abroad as well as at home. If the American system can adapt to include minorities in its midst, it will be better able to cooperate with underdeveloped nations, where the population of "have nots" is even greater. In both cases we must establish an effective way for them to participate.

Transplanting Private Enterprise

American private enterprise must be transplanted and developed in the ghetto, as the *heart* of the ghetto—not to preserve it, not just to provide jobs, but to provide the ghetto nation with the essential requirements for achieving its proportional share in the American business system.

Businesses, the motor forces of American society, must be viably developed where there were no businesses, or only weak ones. They need not be prime natural resource manufacturing corporations at first, but they cannot be the old marginal small businesses. "Mom and Pop" grocery stores are out. Marginal businesses which exploit consumers and workers alike are out. Business and economic development of the ghetto must have a high priority in public policy along with jobs, education, and housing.

Ghetto business development must create new viable businesses and develop older businesses so that they contribute the maximum to community development. This means that minority business must be fully integrated into rebuilt neighborhoods of the inner city, that minority contractors, for example, must obtain a proportionate share of such rebuilding, that minority business must be able to open and expand in the most desirable locations—downtown triple-A rated locations as well as in suburban shopping centers and industrial parks.

Such businesses will provide for many individuals another way out of the ghetto. They will create jobs. They will also provide capital accumulation and the development of a black business manager class. In time, this process will forge the basic economic and social structure that will replace the ghetto as an entity with flourishing new inner cities.

Today many inner cities and their ghetto business communities, ravaged by riots, are commercial ghost towns. Business in the inner city generally is on the decline. Within 30 years, we must build America over again, for because of population growth and physical depreciation, we will need to produce an amount of capital investment equal to all buildings, plant, and equipment now in existence in America.

Yet it is a political and social fact that our cities will not be rebuilt without indigenous economic development, without the active participation of the ghetto nation. For white merchants are simply not investing in the ghetto. They do not find it economically or politically wise. It is thus not feasible for whites to rebuild in the ghettos. Whites are leaving the inner cities and are not returning. The ghetto's 50,000 to 150,000 businesses, many of them inherited from immigrants, serve neither the larger economy nor their own communities very significantly.

The small number of black managers and proprietors testifies to their exclusion from business participation. In 1967, non-whites were 15 per cent of our total population and accounted for 10.8 per cent of all employment. But they are at the bottom of the economic ladder. For example, they comprise 47 per cent of all household service workers. In starkest contrast, in the category of "managers, officials of business, and proprietors," they comprise only 2.7 per cent representation, and the meager total of 209,000. Whites in the same category total 7,286,000.

If non-whites shared proportionally, instead of 209,000 there would be 1,124,000 non-whites in the present total of 7,495,000 of business owners, managers, and officials.

A gross management and ownership gap of more than 900,000 exists. There is thus a prima facie case for bringing more non-whites into small business and management of all kinds if we are to attain anything approaching equal opportunity and participation in business.

Although the category of non-white professionals and technicians has increased, and is increasing at a rate of 11 per cent per year compared with a white increase of 2½ per cent, thus illustrating the educational escape from the ghetto, a business exit hardly exists at all.

Blacks who manage to become proprietors have a very difficult time. According to census figures, the number of proprietors of black businesses has declined since 1950 as the integration and civil rights movement brought them more competition. Restaurants declined 33 per cent; other retail businesses more than 33 per cent; even funeral parlors and barber shops were affected by the trend, declining 6 per cent and 16 per cent respectively. And today the ghetto businessman is being hit up to 25 times harder by crime than his non-ghetto counterpart.

Reflecting the historical neglect, even the actual number of minority and black-owned businesses is difficult to ascertain, for although the agricultural business census enumerates race, the general business census does not. Best estimates are that there are 50,000 to 150,000 non-white businesses in a total business population of 5.2 million, or from 1 to 3 per cent of the total. Proportional participation in business would give minorities 15 per cent of that 5 million, or a total of 750,000—600,000 more than they have now.

Washington, D.C., for example, is 65 per cent black, has a 95 per cent black school population and is, historically, a black cultural center. Yet its black business community numbers less than 8 per cent. Of a total of 28,000 business enterprises, only 2000 are black-owned.

Put another way, one of every 40 whites is a proprietor; only one in about 150 blacks is a proprietor. Such a small participation in business ownership and management indicates the colonial status of the ghetto dweller in our cities.

Of the more than 20 million blacks in America approximately 80 per cent live in urban areas, and of these more than one-third live in the nation's 25 largest cities. The total black market, according to 1965 estimates by the Opinion Research Corporation, is $24 billion a year. Of this market, however, black business serves, at highest estimates, only 10 to 15 per cent. In Harlem, where there are many black owned businesses, 80 to 85 per cent of the gross volume of business is done by white "non-resident" businessmen.

And with high representation in personal services and low representation in contract construction and manufacturing, black businesses are also smaller than businesses owned by whites in the same industries. Best estimates today indicate the following pattern:

	Current Business Population*		
Industry	Total Business	Non-White Owned	Percent Non-White
Contract Construction	500	8	1.6
Manufacturing	330	2	0.7
Personal Services	550	40	7.3
Other Services	550	15	2.8
Retail Trade	2,150	65	3.0
Wholesale Trade	350	5	1.5
All Other	650	15	2.3

* Source: *The American Negro Reference Book*, p. 292.

Note the over-representation in personal services and retail trade. This means that blacks are providing beauty and barbershop services to themselves, in their neighborhoods. Yet even there they do not get a large share of the basic market, such as the food dollars spent by their neighbors. Figures indicate that the black spends only 3 to 4 per cent of his food budget in black-owned stores.

The quality gap has additional implications. Without representation in the manager class and in small business ownership, the ghetto nation as a whole lacks a middle class group to transmit the basic American values of private enterprise by living them.

Recent studies indicate that 4 per cent of all business is located in ghettos of inner cities and that 28 per cent of all businesses are in cities. This means that even if every ghetto business were locally owned, the black would remain under-represented in the business management category.

Another interesting set of figures indicates that even if we achieve total indigenous ownership of the stores in the ghetto, we do not significantly reverse its "balance of payments" problem. The proportion of capital retained by the white store owner and taken out of the ghetto by him, despite claims of militants of "colonialist exploitation," is so small as to be insignificant. In Washington, D.C., according to a recent Federal Trade Commission study, the "foreign" merchant was found to be making 4 per cent, or twice the profit that stores make outside the ghetto. But the money paid by ghetto residents went mainly to pay for goods that were manufactured outside the ghetto. This money flowed back to the manufacturers and others not in the ghetto.

About 38 per cent of the money goes to producers and distributors, 28 per cent to the employees of the stores and 29 per cent for expenses such as advertising, bad debts, and taxes.

This would occur, of course, whether the retail merchant were white or black. "Hire black" and "buy-from-black-suppliers" campaigns such as Operation Breadbasket would, therefore, have more impact than total indigenous ownership. Ownership change must still be accelerated, however, both to make easy the latter processes and for its psychological benefits. The FTC study indicates the necessity for equal business opportunity to be provided beyond the ghetto, in franchising, in joint ventures in larger scale business, and with larger corporations. The minority businessman must be permitted to expand into all areas to achieve equal participation in business, and he must be qualified to face competition from the entire urban market.

A capital gap also exists. Assuming there were 150,000 non-white owned businesses in 1968, and taking into account their industry distribution and typical size, this would represent a total investment in plant, equipment inventory, and working capital of about $5 billion. About 600,000 more businesses would require $20 billion more in capital investment just to bring the ghettos to proportional ownership in line with 1968 totals and sizes of non-white businesses. This should increase, however, at the rate black population increases. If nothing is done, of course, the gap will grow.

We must close the gap, but the present status of the ghetto business community requires that the problems of capital investment and management training be approached in radically new and different ways. Greater risks must be taken and more management assistance must be provided over longer periods of time. The innovations required will be at least as great as the innovations required to develop underdeveloped countries.

For overseas investment the federal government provides insurance, and it is a prime requirement that we insure the risks of ghetto economic development. The Small Business Administration can and does insure the risks. In fact, SBA has the precise instrument needed here—loan guarantee authority—and it needs only maximum utilization. But government power can go only so far. The banking and business communities must become much more involved, to provide a great enough private capital supply and the management assistance and supervision needed. This will require a series of institutional innovations and developments across the entire banking and business sectors.

We must do even more for our minority underdeveloped nation at home than for any foreign country for the obvious reason that we are being forced to do so by events. Urban decay or chaos are the alternatives. The development of the ghetto nation is forced upon us, and it is in our self-interest to respond. But it is also thoroughly justifiable according to basic American principles: to provide the black American and other minorities the birthrights that are being denied them.

Beyond "Equal Opportunity"

Fortunately, we have a newly emerging ethic that takes us beyond equal opportunity. It has both ethical content and operational consequences. We understand today that minorities have handicaps that prevent them from arriving at the starting line ready for fair competition. We know that equal treatment of the obviously unequal can actually be a great injustice. Legal justice is not an issue; essential fairness is. The imposed and cultural handicaps of minorities must be removed.

Israel Zangwill in 1907 said that the ghetto, like slavery, was far more than a legal measure. It had come to exist not only in statutes and and decrees, but in the habits and attitudes of individuals and in the culture of groups. Institutional defects and rascism in our society have stymied the participation of the black entrepreneur and the black businessman, but a whole new generation of black people is seeking its way into American society.

Many, fortunately, now are able to seek the business route that was formerly closed to them. Much of the former civil rights movement is focused upon authentic emancipation through economic development.

We know now that equal opportunity must have realistic and constructive content. It must open a way to liberating self-development. It must provide a place from which to make a contribution, a way to achieve on one's own merits and efforts.

Compensatory Capitalism

If business and industry are to function realistically in this context, I believe we must adapt our institutions so that they develop rather than exclude the minority human resources now so eager to find expression in business.

The new ethic also has operational consequences. Preferential treatment of minorities must be worked out across the entire institutional network of our society. Since capital is so basic, this process must begin in banking, with what I have called "compensatory capitalism." It is already being practiced by the socially and economically aware banking and business communities.

In my work at the Department of Commerce I coordinated the JOBS (Job Opportunities in the Business Sector) program with the National Alliance of Businessmen. Similarly, when I went to the Small Business Administration I found that several responses were already being made by banks, business, and government, but greater national leadership and expanded business-like approaches were needed to bring minorities into the enterprise system.

Some bankers have already begun to accept the principle of less stringent requirements for loans to minorities, with, to be sure, the same risk guarantees we have when we lend to underdeveloped nations. This easing of requirements in lending is a basic social-economic principle behind compensatory capitalism. If banks do not accept this they are not going to make loans to the minorities. But banks accept its social justification, for it is in the American tradition to compensate in one way or another for differentials of inheritance or environment that lessen an individual's fundamental right to participate in our society.

In education, for example, we accept as a nation the idea that every individual has a basic right to develop to his maximum potential. For those disadvantaged whose environment deprives them of a quality education we devised a system of compensatory education (Head Start). Although we have not fully executed it yet, we have begun to create special educational programs to counteract the deprivation which has been the lot of the disadvantaged. Head Start is only one successful example. This form of compensation acknowledges the right of each child to develop fully. It is both morally right and economically sound.

We have also provided compensatory programs for those who have lacked the opportunity to develop usable vocational skills. A variety of government-sponsored programs of training and re-training is available through the Manpower Development and Training Act. This form of compensation acknowledges everybody's right to the dignity of useful work, and recognizes the need for the American government to provide leadership both in motivation and in training —to make it possible for the disadvantaged to develop the skills required to work in this modern era.

We acknowledge the right to develop oneself to the maximum in employment. We acknowledge as a nation the basic right of all to work or to be educated to an employable level. Compensatory training programs enable disadvantaged citizens to enter and compete fairly in the labor market. Compensatory capitalism, therefore, simply provides basic support for the private enterprise system and for American democracy.

Dimensions of a Compensatory Program

Since what is at issue is the economic base of democracy, a program of "coping with the problem" such as welfare, will not do the job. What we need is a full-scale, national commitment, complete with timetable, and a combined public-private effort to bring minorities into proportional business participation in America. Equal opportunity and integration are not enough. What must be sought is participation in the system on an equal basis. How well we can achieve this, moreover, can be measured.

QUANTITY AND EQUALITY

The objectives of such an effort are continuing increases in numbers, sizes, and quality of minority businesses. In the manpower area, the number of proprietors, managers, and business officials must increase similarly, so that they will be able to qualify for advancement in big business as well as small. The capital requirement is that sufficient investment is channeled into ghetto economic development so that the ghetto can be "developed" out of existence. And it must all be done in time to be of substantial effect in halting urban stagnation or chaos.

INNOVATION IS NEEDED

Compensatory capitalism must, therefore, meet not only the capital requirement of its mission, but its management training and technical assistance requirements as well. It requires many innovations in the field of management and entrepreneur training.

It may require new forms of the enterprise, some of which are already being proposed in the Community Self-Determination Bill in Congress, which is described in chapter 3 by John McClaughry.

If we are serious about this, public and private sources to pioneer in the field must found a national clearing house for ghetto economic research and development—and by development I mean the development of cost-effective program solutions.

ENTREPRENEUR TRAINING

We really know very little about entrepreneur training. For example, in Washington it falls between and among the functions of five different agencies. There is little or no initiative and experiment to produce new forms of entrepreneur training. Yet entrepreneur training may yield higher social economic "payoffs" than any other form of training the government could fund.

Were the problem of ghetto economic development a defense and space problem, we would have vast research development studies and projects planned and underway for the next five to 20 years. Crash programs should be underway. We must do no less for economic development. A systematic approach can begin at any time. With only a small task force working on it today we have already come up with the outlines of a 20-year program which could substantially reduce the size of the problem.

If past trends continue the business population will increase from about 5.3 million today to about 7 million in 1988. If blacks remain at 15 per cent of the population, parity would require more than 1,050,000 black businesses. An average increase of 40,000 new black businesses a year is therefore required.

This figure however, is *net*. Each year nine per cent of all businesses are new, and eight per cent of all businesses are discontinued, so the total is growing at only a one per cent rate. In 1968, it is estimated, there were 450,000 new starts, 394,000 businesses discontinued, for a net increase of 56,000.

It is hard to estimate how many new businesses would be required for minority-owned businesses to achieve parity in 20 years. Little data is available on the life expectancy of minority businesses. But success will depend on the development of a creative program to provide training and managerial assistance. A plan for such a managerial assistance program organized on a national level, not unlike the National Alliance of Businessmen, is needed. I recommended such a program to President Nixon in January, 1969.

In 1968 the SBA, through its direct loan and loan guarantee programs, aided 1,700 minority-owned businesses. Under Project OWN, which I initiated in August, 1968, while at the SBA, by December we were making loans to minority-owned businesses at an annual rate of 5,000.

Realistically filling the capital gap also requires that we take into account the limitations as well as the opportunities that are present. Since 60 per cent of all American business is retail, it may be assumed that the bulk of minority businesses will be in that area. The amount of money required to go into these businesses on a sound basis is today approximately $30,000. If the borrower provides $10,000, and $20,000 comes from government and private sources, $4.4 billion would be needed annually for full parity, $2.2 billion for 50 per cent parity, less what is paid back each year in interest and principal.

If the average loan was for 10 years, a bit less than one-half of these sums would be required over 20 years. On the average the gross sums required would be $2 billion and $1 billion. Assuming an SBA-type revolving ghetto business development fund, larger sums would be needed at first, and the need would decline later. If only loan guarantees are employed, SBA will have to put aside $200 million annually to achieve full parity, and $100 million annually for the 50 per cent of parity goal.

For larger businesses which would be within the capability of growing minority communities to develop, larger financings would be available through ordinary channels. As communities reach the equivalent of take-off point to becoming self-sustaining, all the normal channels from which they have been excluded, or were incapable of participating in, would be opened.

What is needed is the catalytic development effort of compensatory capitalism to promote effective business workings between the system and minorities.

BANKS

Banks are already on the way in their practice of compensatory capitalism. The leadership of such banks as the First Pennsylvania Banking and Trust Company is well documented and is being duplicated throughout the country. The American Bankers Association is already committed to doing business with the ghetto nation not just as individuals but as business owners and managers.

The willingness of banks to participate and embrace, with government support, the principles of compensatory capitalism, was demonstrated during the first seven months of Project OWN. With the SBA guaranteeing 90 per cent of the loans, banks increased their rate of loans to minority-owned businesses by more than 800 per cent. By January 1969, almost two-thirds of all SBA loans to minority businesses were being made through the banks, compared to almost none prior to Project OWN.

RETAILING AND CONSTRUCTION

A full scale, well developed program with continuing research can identify the best fields for minority entrepreneurs. It is already apparent, for example, that the construction industry presents an important opportunity area for minority business growth.

INDUSTRY AND TRADE ASSOCIATIONS

Industry and trade associations are becoming involved. The Menswear Retailers of America has committed both money and talent. They are using the facilities of their 3,300 member national trade association in a joint program with leading manufacturers to create ownership opportunities for minority group members. Manufacturers have pledged $20 million of extended credit for these new stores. The Retailers now have a full-time employee seeking minority entrepreneurs, selecting locations, negotiating leases or buyouts, and identifying a local member of the Retailers to serve as a specialist-counselor for each new minority entrepreneur.

By taking these simple steps, the Retailers are leading the way in making the appropriate institutional responses to the demand by minorities for access to "a piece of the action" and a chance to achieve based on one's talents and efforts. The Retailers' imaginative work needs duplication by every trade association and its industrial suppliers.

FRANCHISING

Franchises also present a valuable opportunity for minorities, and have the advantage of a built-in system of management supervision and training. SBA has developed a program with franchisors that will enable SBA to lend money or guarantee loans almost concurrently with the franchiser's selection of a qualified minority franchisee.

COMMUNITY ORGANIZATIONS

Moderate or militant community organizations of minority groups across the country, from Harlem to Nagadocshes, from Watts to Washington, are today investigating how far they can go in rebuilding their communities, and developing themselves in the basic business disciplines of the free private enterprise system.

In the fall of 1968 about 40 groups and national organizations from the minority community, from most militant to most moderate, attended a meeting of the Black Economic Development Advisory group at SBA. A week later, about 40 more black and white representatives of groups, many of them sponsored by our largest corporations which are engaged in one form or another in minority economic development, also met. Heartened at the response the business community and their governments are making, the minorities were eager to cooperate and suggested that they organize to provide advice and contacts to all agencies and groups which would listen to them.

Project OWN

I was sworn in as Administrator of the SBA in July of 1968, and charged by the President with the responsibility of greatly increasing loans to minority businesses. It quickly became apparent that these loans could not be made without accepting some new lending principles that took into account the higher risks and general lack of capital in the minority community. Thus was born the principle of compensatory capitalism, which is based on the premise that higher risks can be accepted when higher priority social objectives are at stake. In August 1968, with the cooperation of the banks, we initiated Project OWN.

Project OWN's record of success is clear. In fiscal year 1968, the SBA made loans of $30 million to the minority community. Under Project OWN, and even with cuts of two-thirds in the SBA loan budget, the annual loan rate to minority-owned businesses between August and December 1968 had leaped to $100 million. It had been the goal of Project OWN that by 1971, with a national program of technical and managerial assistance supported by American business, the loan rate to minorities could move up to $500 million. If this rate were continued for 20 years the gap between the percentage of minority-owned businesses and their percentage of the population would be drastically closed.

A program embracing the principle of compensatory capitalism involves taking higher risks, and this obviously means higher loss rates. Normal loss rates on loans to white-owned businesses were 2.8 per cent. Actuarial studies done for the SBA estimate that the loss rate to minority-owned businesses would be approximately 12 per cent. Let us suppose that the annual level of loans to minority-owned businesses were at $500 million, and that the loss rate was even as high as 15 per cent. This would entail losses of $75 million per year—the cost of re-equipping one Polaris submarine for multiple warheads. Surely $75 million is a reasonable price to pay to help commercially rebuild our cities and give minority communities a stake in the free enterprise system. It could even be argued that the increase in tax revenues from the 85 per cent of the businesses that do succeed will more than compensate for the loss, not to mention the social benefits our society will derive from this investment.

Anyone who listens cannot mistake the loudest cry from the ghetto today. It is for ownership, for participation. It is a cry of anger and frustration at being unable to share in the basic American dream of ownership. It was a dream like this that brought so many immigrants to these shores, that brought them from poverty, to security, to affluence. Ownership of a part of American business can help bring the black American and other minority citizens into full partnership in America. It can generate pride and responsibility. It can help make our cities fit places in which to live.

The minority community is demanding not just a voice, but substance, an economic stake in free enterprise, to be risked, to gain or to lose, and thereby share in the adventure and rewards of a truly free society. They cannot demand more; nor can we afford to provide less.

A. Wright Elliott *

6

"Black Capitalism" and the Business Community

Before becoming too deeply immersed in the troubled waters of "black capitalism," it would be wise to dispense with rhetorical and semantic games and agree upon a definition of terms.

We must go beyond simplistic slogans and admit that what we are really talking about is *ways that blacks can legitimately acquire a larger stake in our society*. In the economic sense, this means that they must legitimately acquire and control more resources. The concept of private property, which is a major foundation of capitalism, offers no support for color prejudice or special advantage.

We are suggesting, then, that before we proceed any further, we attempt to spell out just what business is being asked to get into. Far more questions will be raised than answered; but in large part we perceive this—the posing of critical questions—as our primary task.

Let it be clear, however, that we are not in any way questioning either the presence or the severity of a critical national problem. Nor are we in any way suggesting that business should not be involved in the implementation of solutions to this and other problems that we have traditionally labeled as "social."

What we are saying is: when so many people's lives—and indeed, perhaps the very life of our society—are at stake, let us be as certain as we can that we know what we are about.

A. Wright Elliott *is senior vice president of the Program Planning Division of the National Association of Manufacturers.*

* *This paper was prepared with the cooperation of Paul Slater, Director, Urban Affairs Study Group, National Association of Manufacturers.*

"Black" vs. Traditional Capitalism

No one knows better than a successful American industrialist the traditional meaning and function of capitalism. But is there a change when the word "black" is inserted in front? The business community, as well as the black community, must be alerted to the fact that, even if the name of the game has been changed only slightly, the game itself will very probably be played according to a different set of rules.

A New Jersey newspaper editorial trying to explain what blacks are really seeking notes that ". . . militants are calling for black capitalism, for the creation of self-contained, self-supporting economies inside the Negro community."

Is this where "black capitalism" is? A brief scanning of the public utterances of a number of black leaders may shed further light. Roy Innis, of CORE, sees black capitalism as a way for Negroes "to get control over the institutions that we have to live with." And the Reverend Franklin Florence, of Rochester's FIGHTON (a black company in Rochester established with white business support and described in chapter 12 by Martin Skala), in emphasizing the demand for economic self-sufficiency of the Negro community, stresses that the concept of black capitalism he advocates does not involve independent businessmen, even if they are Negro. He states: "Community organization is the important thing, and FIGHTON is owned by the community."

Burkeley Burrell, of the National Business League, suggests that by means of major corporations going into the ghetto, "a system of plantationships that is hated will be destroyed." Further, "What is needed is partnership. We seek (and demand) an equal or better sharing of ownership and operation of the business and commerce of the ghetto. A majority of the business community, as a matter of re-enlightened self-interest, must provide the equity, capital resources, technical capability, guidance, and support that are essential to the growth and development of inter-racial business within the central city."

And, of course, the subject of intensive development of the black community has raised its own storm among Negro thinkers. To Dr. Kenneth Clark, for one, it leads to a "gilded ghetto" and, what is worse, to a separate society. Whitney Young, of the National Urban League, feels that "black capitalism" is simply a slogan, and that there is actually no such thing as black capitalism, any more than white capitalism, in concept or reality. Young states that the "concept of encouraging black entrepreneurship [helping black people become managers and stockholders in business] is sound." But, to Young, as to Clark, the term black capitalism implies a separateness: a "black" and a "white" economy, a concept with which he takes sharp issue.

What, then, of the ". . . creation of self-contained, self-supporting economies inside the Negro community?" If this is what black capitalism means, to at least a number of key black leaders, what role does this imply for the majority white community, particularly its business leadership? Do blacks want them for it, against it, or neutral? And if "for it," what are the specifics of "mutuality," i.e., who gives what, and how, and what is received in return?

Apparently at least one group of United States Senators, including Jacob Javits, Charles Percy, Fred Harris and Gaylord Nelson, together with a number of top business leaders, seem already to have resolved this question, coming down squarely in favor of the version of black capitalism in the ghettos that is spelled out in the "Community Self-Determination Act of 1968," described by John McClaughry in chapter 3.

On the face of it, one might have expected their endorsement to be met with unbounded enthusiasm on the part of the more militant blacks. Yet, at a meeting in Washington, D.C., in December, 1968, the Reverend Franklin Florence of Rochester, New York, among other black leaders, expressed serious reservations about this bill. In fact, Florence openly called it a "hypocritical piece of legislation," and suggested that it be "torn up, because you can't start wrong and end right." He held that the legislation would set up "Mickey Mouse" types of organizations, instead of giving control to the local leaders responsive to ghetto needs: "The problem of the ghetto is powerlessness; if the people there don't have the power to negotiate for themselves, there will be no economic development."

Another critic, Benjamin Wright, chairman of a new action committee of Negro business leaders, called for a moratorium on the bill until the goals for black self-determination could be established by blacks themselves. Leading black managers of local economic development corporations charged that certain Negro interests would use economic development to meet their own self-serving political needs, and let "enterprise-building go to hell." For our own part, one of the tough philosophical dilemmas is this: Are we willing to accept separate but equal economic development, if in fact it leads the nation toward apartheid?

Along this same line, one further question must be raised: When we talk about economic development, are we really discussing the development of *political* vehicles in black communities, aimed toward the assumption of political power; or are we discussing economic instruments, designed to assume economic power? For these are quite different considerations. One can develop political instrumentalities that have nothing to do with economic enterprise. And if this is our goal, let us make it clear to all, black and white, that the development of business entities is, at best, a secondary consideration.

Finally, there is the whole question of the community corporation as a business model. One would hope for example that those black leaders who are calling for "Mom and Pop" to invest $5.00 a month in ghetto community corporations would also, at the same time, explain to "Mom and Pop" what $5.00 worth of a healthy common stock, invested in 1960, would be worth today.

What we are saying is that "Pop" should have the option, in a truly free society, to put his money where he pleases, and ideally, to be informed about, and therefore to truly have as many choices as possible.

If, in fact, community corporations are therefore to devote a certain percentage of gross or net profits to be invested in "social or supportive services" for the community as a whole, we would also hope—indeed, one should insist—the community be aware that not all corporations succeed and that in marginal years the supportive services may be non-existent.

All of which may get us closer to "where it really is" today: a concept still beset by criticisms, doubts, and dilemmas on all sides.

THE NEW GAME: AN ALTERED SET OF RULES

In order to make some sense with regard to a definition of black capitalism, we might begin by considering what has happened in the area of employment. For in this area, where the business community and the black community have already interacted for an extended period of time, we have learned a great deal that can be useful for the questions posed by ghetto entrepreneurship.

With the major push launched by the National Alliance of Businessmen, some 100,000 minority group persons were gainfully employed in industry in 1968 alone. As the tempo of hiring increased and as companies learned to build in the requisite supports necessary to effectively employ and retain disadvantaged persons, the charge of "reverse discrimination" arose more than once from members of the non-black work force.

In response to this charge, many companies have attempted to educate their employees on the "new facts of life"—namely, that special corporate efforts must be made to help the new minority workers because of the deficits, resulting from life-long discrimination, with which they enter the labor market. The case has already been successfully made that such special efforts are necessary ("compensatory capitalism," chapter 5), in order to bring employees from the hard-core up to that point where they can successfully compete, at which time the "unequal support" can be discontinued.

By the same token, efforts to help blacks become successful entrepreneurs will obviously require other "special supports"—in terms of financial, managerial, and technical assistance—so that black entrepreneurs, in most instances lacking a history of business involvement and experience, may be helped to compete on equal terms.

But, if this need be done, if the rules must be altered (and we think they must), does this not have serious implications for *existing* small companies, whether owned and managed by blacks or whites, currently struggling to stay alive and healthy? How will these companies perceive these special supports? For years, they have been told that "competition is the name of the game," that "nice guys finish last"; but now, certain new, smaller companies will be receiving special help to assist them toward eventual success in the market place. There have already been some cries of "foul" from those in established-but-marginal businesses who have never received special supports.

Has the impact of this problem really been considered? Have we learned anything, hopefully, from our minority employment efforts? Should we really move into high gear, helping minority group members establish businesses in significant numbers across the country, before we have articulated well-reasoned answers to the charges of special privilege?

We would suggest that, again, as with programs to hire the hard-core, some type of arrangement will probably have to be worked out to help balance the competitive situation between the less successful established enterprises and their new competitors. Companies employing the hard-core are finding that, in the end, it is *more productive* (i.e. profit-oriented) to demonstrate additional concern for the entire work force, in order to forestall dissension.

Moving on, let us look for a moment at the demands of many of the black separatists. What they seem to want from the major corporations is, quite simply and bluntly, capital. They want either direct loans to assist in establishing black-owned enterprises, or capital investments in ghetto facilities to establish initially white-owned enterprises which will, after a designated period of time, be divested with regard to majority ownership.

What then is corporate management really being asked to do? To (1) invest capital in a highly risky venture with a return much lower than normal if analyzed in terms of the degree of risk; (2) train black managers and employees, thereby—to judge by a wealth of empirical data—requiring a higher than normal expenditure for training and a consequent reduction in net profit in the earlier years; (3) provide continuing technical management assistance to the new corporation.

And what can the investing company expect to receive in return? Simply this: once the new corporation becomes successful and in a position to begin to generate a return on the invested risk capital, the investing company is asked to divest ownership—or at least, to relinquish a majority position.

Realistically, of course, the major corporations are not investing this capital for the *primary* purpose of capital return. What they are hoping to "buy" (and we must be totally honest about it) is a long-range social harmony, whereby twenty years from now their companies will exist in a climate as free as possible from upheaval and disruption. Or to state it positively, they will thus exist in a climate where economic integration has led to the fullest participation of all of our citizens, regardless of color, in our national prosperity.

Capitalism? Not really, not in the sense of the term as it is applied in this country today. But if a relatively small investment today serves to protect the overall economic and political system—if, in the long-run, our traditional system survives as a result of this investment—then perhaps what we are talking about is little different from an investment in new plant, or new equipment, or an investment in middle-management education. That is, it can be compared to an expenditure for long-term corporate improvement.

Parenthetically, any definition of capitalism in the "purest" sense is open to question. There are numerous instances of government subsidies to the profit-making sector, for example, that make the process of definition a difficult one. In short, discarding any glib definition is there a difference between capitalism and "black capitalism"? Are we not talking really about making the benefits of our capitalistic system more accessible to the black community, full well recognizing the concomitant benefits to the *total* society?

This would seem to suggest, then, that this form of corporate investment in the future is not only required but legitimate to the interests of the stockholders of major corporations. It suggests something else as well: Such investments could qualify for special consideration within a broadened concept which might be called "Social Cost-Accounting."

Capital investment by business corporations can do much to overcome and rectify past inequities to the black community, partially through assisting in the development of Negro-owned and Negro-managed enterprises. Therefore, some incentive, some allowance, (some "social-credit,") might be allowed. As an example, we must, at the least, intensively study proposals that would provide a tax credit to corporations that establish ghetto facilities.

The remainder of this chapter will be devoted to a description of where we feel both the black community and the business community are; and more important, to some tentative suggestions as to where the two must go—together.

The Business Community: A Hard Look at Its Role

To begin, what must the business community do if it is to assist the development of black business enterprise?

First, the white business community must honestly assess the differences that exist between it and the black business community. It must admit that, with few exceptions, it is technologically far more advanced; it possesses far more capital; it currently has a much larger pool of managerial talent than is generally available in the black community.

It must recognize that there are currently relatively few people in the black community who are fully prepared to build and manage enterprises—without some assistance; and finally that this gap between black and white America must be closed, employing as high a degree of problem-solving creativity as business has ever displayed in the past.

We face a significant national problem, one that demands special solutions. Therefore, rigidity in thought, as well as in action, is virtually intolerable. This means the business community must look honestly at such concepts as "sheltered markets," which guarantee the survival of a newly-launched enterprise for a stated period of time. It means that business must invest heavily in education and training, with a different reading of the balance sheet.

An initial decision has to be made as to the particular goal a given company wishes to achieve in its relationship with the black business community. Should the company consider opening a branch operation in the ghetto staffed by minority group members? Set up an operation with the avowed purpose of turning it over to the black community as soon as indigenous staff can be trained to run the firm? Or provide managerial and technical assistance to on-going black firms, in the process of developing necessary expertise? Obviously, the problem is not simply the typical case of how the company best maximizes profits. To enter into many minority communities today is comparable, virtually, to crossing an international border. Failure to consider the impact of this move on the ghetto inhabitants is comparable, in business terms, to ignoring the marketing function completely.

And simply to give in to the most insistent minority voice (or group) on the matter of participation may be, in the end, the most costly and least productive way to proceed. The decision must take into account the needs of *both* the company and the community. In the end, a cooperative relationship between the black and white business worlds is vital if long-term results are to be productive.

Another important point must be made with regard to the white business community. It is unfortunate, but probably true, that most businessmen, when they leave the making of cars, steel, or computers in order to serve on the board of non-profit or voluntary agencies, somehow manage to leave behind at the office their hard-nosed pragmatism—to leave behind the rigorous questions as to performance and achievement that make their companies successful and viable entities.

Nothing could be worse for the black capitalism effort, in which white businessmen are needed as *businessmen*. What must be brought to bear in this task is the best of our management tools, but, even more important, the best of the proved managerial attitudes.

Much will have to be "given," regardless of the terms of giving, and there is an obvious danger that the white business community runs the risk of becoming collectively "social workers in disguise." If it lends too much managerial assistance, and for too long; if the "sheltered market" ("in-house" contracts) stays sheltered, beyond judicious limits; if capital is repeatedly lent, in spite of continued non-achievement, over too long a period of time (that is, without regard to the discipline required of profit-making) then, we may find ourselves in the process of creating merely a new state of dependency—in which the black man finds himself permanently dependent upon the business loan and the borrowed executive consultant instead of on the welfare check and the case worker.

The Black Community: A "Quid Pro Quo"

Black leadership must make the same recognition of the gap—financial, technological, and experimental—that currently exists between white and black America. Which is to say, it must perceive and acknowledge the need to close the gap, hence the need for white "things," white experience, white personnel.

With the wholly honest admission that the white businessman has much to gain both from the ensuing relationship and from the programs that will be generated as the commitment is translated into reality, we must be frank to admit a bias. It is simply this: that this mutuality of interest demands interdependence, rather than independence. This assumes, as firmly as we can put it, that separation of the races in this country *cannot* be the ultimate goal toward which these efforts are directed. This is not to say that there is anything, whatsoever, wrong with the development of black-owned and black-managed enterprise; nor does it imply that American industry should not participate in the implementation of such efforts. But it must be stated forthrightly that the development of black-owned and black-managed enterprise is quite a different thing from the development of independent black communities.

In short, the ultimate goal must be integration, with economic development, or black capitalism, being only one vehicle toward that goal. We need—indeed, we must have—a unified, not a divided society. The hope is that economic development efforts may be one, and only one, of many interdependent arrangements that serve as programmatic devices in this crucial movement toward unification.

What else are we asking of the black community? That it must be as flexible and open to experimentation as the white business community. This means that we should not decide on a single model, if it implies rejecting all others; this means we must not impose one set of criteria as we make decisions, that we must allow diversity in our programming as well as in our conceptualization. For if the black community were to demand that one model, and one model alone, would suffice, it would indicate an overt rejection of capitalism. For it would strike at the essence of the concept of the marketplace, which permits, indeed encourages, as many models as possible to be provided a chance to succeed, and a chance to fail. In practical terms, this means that such existing organizations as ICBIF, a black-managed business development corporation in Detroit; FIGHTON, the community corporation in Rochester; the Reverend Sullivan's innovative OIC development in Philadelphia—all of these experimental models described in chapter 12 by Mr. Skala must be given their day in the sun. So must all attempts to encourage "normal" black enterprise, totally *unrelated* to community corporations and the like.

And we are saying also that we cannot reject the "Mom and Pop" store as one viable model. For if "Pop" decides to launch a new venture, a neighborhood laundry in Harlem, who can be presumptuous enough to say—and according to what higher moral or economic order—that "Pop" should not be given this option—and that the option should not be programmed for. It is one thing to say that "our goal" is to build a black General Motors by the year 2000. It is quite another, however, to prohibit everyone (including "Pop's" laundry) from trying to accomplish the same according to his own version of what the "good life" is really all about.

And somehow, in all the talk about the economic development of the ghetto and the growth of black entrepreneurship, the consumer has largely been left out. This, we believe, is a short-sighted and perilous neglect. For unless we are mistaken, this in the final analysis is what the whole discussion is about—that is, all efforts to strengthen and build the capacity of the business community in the ghetto are aimed at strengthening and building the capacity of the *individuals* making up the ghetto.

If we enter the arena of black capitalism with the idea of remaining flexible, of maximizing alternatives, we allow for the emergence of a large number of *individual* black capitalists in the years ahead. Indeed, this suggests the development of a far stronger, and more dynamic, black middle class than is apt to develop under the restriction of a single, rigid model.

Mutuality: The Ultimate Challenge

One thing is certain, and it needs little elaboration: If black-white business interaction is to succeed, there must be trust, there must be openness, there must be a climate that makes "leveling" easy (as easy as it can ever be). The time for "playing games" is indeed over.

There must be, flowing out of this climate of trust, a spirit of accommodation, of useful compromise, of negotiation. For if we really believe in a mutuality of interest, this means each of us has something to gain, and at the same time, something very precious to lose.

Perhaps this is at the essence of what "black capitalism" truly means, for it is here that the concepts, when tested, must really work. There are products, or values, to be "sold" by both black and white alike, and at the same time, both are consumers for those products. In short, we are in the marketplace, where love and admiration are desirable but not crucial, where a relationship of trust can be based on mutual self-interest, on a bargaining process in which there are potential benefits for all parties. This is where we are; if we can accept it as an encounter in the marketplace, then we can begin; that in itself implies a commitment to try.

A final word: At the heart of what we have attempted to say is a deep awareness of both the urgency of the problem and the great opportunity that is present. The effective involvement of Negroes with the business establishment is one vital element of a national effort to resolve our most profound domestic crisis.

And yet, if only because of this urgency, there is the danger that, plugging in quickly without comprehending the complexity of the problem, we would find that we have invested heavily in time, money, and emotion, without a sufficiently meaningful return. This is not to say that we should sit back and wait for the results of further surveys and studies. To the contrary, we would agree that the ghettos have had, if anything, too many studies, and far too little action. We are suggesting, however, that as we proceed we work double time at understanding what it is that both the ghetto residents and the business community need and are asking for—so that we might determine how we can best mutually use our resources to fulfill those needs.

Of one thing we are certain: Negroes in this country must have their rightful place at last in the processes of capitalism, and reap the rewards that come with greater involvement, if we are to have a truly free and just society.

*Peter F. McNeish**

7

Where Does the Money Come From?

The Roots of Deficiency

One of the toughest urban challenges facing the banking industry is the assurance of adequate financing to business enterprises within the inner city. The continuing growth of urban blight and the growing demand for economic participation from residents of ghetto communities attest to the fact that public effort alone—which is typical of those efforts predating the period of civil disorders—has not been able to reverse the deterioration of the ghettos. Yet private capital, which originally built these cities, has been drawn into development of the inner city far less than it should have been.

THE FANTASY OF CREDIT FLIGHT

Because in recent years the limited flow of capital to inner cities has become more prominent as the problems of these areas have become magnified, financial institutions are often accused of consciously perpetuating inner-city deterioration and the dehumanizing conditions which exist there. This belief is fiction, not fact.

The underlying factors which, in fact, cause the existence of a "credit deficiency" environment must be recognized and understood. Underemployment, a consequent fluctuating income base, low-quality

---

Formerly urban advisor to the Pennsylvania Department of Community Affairs and director of the Office of Economic Opportunity of that state, PETER F. MCNEISH *is executive secretary, Committee on Urban Affairs, American Bankers Association. He has served on a number of committees and councils dealing with state, urban and federal problems.*

* *Mr. McNeish acknowledges the research assistance of Mr. Sherwood T. Small in the preparation of this chapter.*

education and educational facilities, inadequate transportation, deteriorated housing, a poor quality of public services, and a host of related market factors are the reasons why credit and investment capital have been slow to find their way into the ghetto. There is a direct and indisputable relationship between the economic base of any given area and the allocation of credit and investment capital to it. The simple fact is that the inner-city ghetto areas do not have the essential market characteristics necessary to bid effectively for capital in the market as we know it.

ULTIMATE SOLUTIONS OR ACTION NOW

The ultimate solution to this problem will not be provided by simply infusing substantial amounts of capital into areas which lack the essential socio-economic base to support and sustain growth. To attain real results, the vital fabric of the inner city must be improved. Assured employment, increased income levels, the provision of quality education and training—such factors will help to cure credit and investment capital concerns more quickly than artificial devices or intravenous feeding.

We clearly recognize, however, that the realities of urban America today demand we take action now, and not wait for ultimate solutions. Moreover, it would be grossly misleading to suggest that the inner city is totally without a resource base of any substance whatever. There is within the ghetto an undeveloped resource of human talent, energy, and ambition, an underdeveloped but increasingly effective purchasing power, an underutilized capacity for business development, latent market potential, the capacity for leadership, and an untested opportunity for growth. Consequently, affirmative actions are both possible and necessary.

Using Traditional Capital Sources

CREDIT CRITERIA

If one attempts to apply traditional credit analysis techniques to the problem of business development in the ghetto community, the analysis bogs down at a very early stage. Business loans are made on the basis of an established set of criteria, including: the competence and character of management; potential for stability or growth of earnings; growth in sales; quality of assets; comparative operating ratios; past performance on loans; the amount of personal equity in initial capitalization; and the amount and quality of market competition. Yet in the case of the ghetto community's economy, many of the factors required to meet these essential criteria may be lacking.

An individual's past performance on loans may show a record of some delinquency or an occasional write-off which makes the lending officer's justification of the new loan extremely difficult. Or the quality of the business's fixed assets may be obsolete or in poor working order, which again complicates the lending decision, since the assets cannot be used as security for the loan. The nature of the enterprise may be that sales are extremely volatile, and lending institutions may be skeptical about the stability of such ventures.

Oftentimes the ghetto businessman is attempting to compete with larger and more sophisticated companies in the same market arena. Even though his product or service might be superior in quality, he may lack the skills to market his goods, or his price may be far above that of his competitor due to his small volume and average unit cost of production. Thus, even if one discounts any problems of prejudicial attitude, inherent business risks may be present, and for sound business reasons the lender may determine he cannot justify an extension of credit.

RISK AND RATE OF RETURN

From the bank's economic point of view an additional restraining consideration is the adequacy of rate of return in relation to risk. In many cases, there is simply no interest rate that can be legally charged for high risk loans which will adequately compensate the lender. While an effective rate of 25–30 per cent might be considered commensurate with risk from the lender's point of view, not only are such rates prohibited by law in all states but they also would place an unconscionable and unrealistic repayment schedule on the borrower's shoulders. Yet, every lender must continuously consider its responsibility to produce a profit for its investor-stockholders and its fiduciary responsibilities to its depositors and the public. These factors, together with strongly competing demands for funds in today's tight money markets place the ghetto business community in a highly non-competitive posture. Moreover, such loans have typically been small in size with disproportionately high servicing costs—still another factor which will dissuade lending officers from "distorting" their aggregate loan portfolios with any volume of such high risk paper.

ATTITUDE OF LENDERS

Finally, there is the issue of attitude on the part of the lending fraternity. Seasoned lending officers skilled in analyzing business credit needs are not normally expected to evaluate the potential trade-offs between economic and social costs and benefits. Given an economically bankable situation, they can easily develop the analysis and reach a loan decision. In dealing with business applicants from the ghetto community, however, negative past experiences, non-applicability of social benefit criteria, and, in some cases, prejudice are all factors which influence attempts at objective analysis.

THE SOCIAL FUNCTION OF CREDIT

In theory, banks as multi-purpose lenders fulfill their economic function when funds are channeled into those sectors where the need is greatest—and need is traditionally measured by market demand, i.e. price. But such theory does not satisfy those who today are wrestling with the problems of rebuilding our inner cities or providing capital to support minority entrepreneurship. The fact of the matter is that while making capital available for such efforts may not be justified on the basis of pure economics, it is quite important for the long-run stability of our communities and our nation that ways be devised to obtain the funds needed to meet our most pressing social problems.

Recent Approaches

Bankers are developing a deep interest in providing solutions to these problems. Several new approaches have been designed to help channel funds into areas where the social need—as opposed to purely economic demand—of the market place is greatest. Such programs are receiving the increasing attention of individual bankers as well as of banker associations. They recognize, of course, that frequently credit must be advanced at less than normal yield, and with more than normal risk and effort.

In some instances the lending activity of commercial banks for minority-group or ghetto community business ventures is handled in the normal course of business with yield as the prime motivating force and degree of risk on a par with the bank's other business loans. In a number of other cases where banks provided working capital for minority entrepreneurs the loans were made at market yields. And although lenders may have had certain initial reservations concerning the risk involved, their delinquency and default experience has been generally as good as the institution's average.

RATIONALE FOR INVOLVEMENT

Many of the institutions now involved in this field, however, also are concerned with important but less immediately tangible rewards, some of which are considered vital enough to justify taking below-market yields or above average risks. These include a long-range view by some lenders that minority group business enterprises and individual accounts constitute a potential market of substantial proportions, particularly in view of the expectation of substantial rise in income levels of these residents. Thus, penetration of new markets takes on significance, particularly for those institutions whose market area is constricted by legal limitation. In some cities, particularly those where tensions have not yet reached a critical stage, lenders have adopted a constructive policy toward business loans in the ghetto communities as a preventive strategy. In other communities, top executives of lending institutions have taken an even broader view that a metropolitan area cannot remain healthy with a rotting core. Their lending efforts for business enterprises and housing, together with related programs to improve employment opportunities, education, transportation and the like, are considered as foundation stones for the economic revival of their cities.

ACTION PROGRAMS

Numerous investment plans and economic programs have been suggested to speed the flow of capital to the ghetto; several have moved past the proposal stage, been implemented and produced measurable benefits. Variations on locus of initiative, perceived rewards and methodology of operation have been numerous.

Unilateral Bank Action—One such program involves unilateral action by banks in a direct action program with the ghetto community and its business development potential. The bank simply makes a decision that it is to its own long-run advantage to re-examine its credit policy toward "marginal" loans for minority group businessmen. Often this decision will be prompted by recognition that the inner city and its minority community is a significant segment of the bank's principal market, and that the bank should begin to meet the needs of the participants in that market area.

One example of this type of direct action is the program of the First Pennsylvania Banking and Trust Company of Philadelphia initiated in early 1967 when the bank actively began to seek out potential minority businessmen and help them develop a financial foothold in their businesses. A major factor in the program's favorable reception was senior management's aggressive commitment to the program's objective—to help the inner city regain its status as a viable economy (See chapter 12).

To people long familiar with the syndrome of welfare, corporate charity, etc., this was a welcome change, since it offered a segment of the community a chance to stand on its own and be measured by its economic achievement instead of a social worker's yardstick. A second and equally important factor was the selection of a particular group of bank personnel to administer the program. Instead of relying on senior management, the bank went to its younger officers and trainees who, although schooled in the bank's credit analysis techniques, could examine such loans with some detachment from institutional biases. These younger managers also had the potential to more easily develop a rapport with the black community and eliminate much of the distrust the community has long had toward lending institutions. In addition, loan decisions took into consideration a combination of economic and non-economic factors. Oftentimes a man's character, sincerity, and knowledge of his skill would become equally important as his past credit record.

Special Loan Fund—Another type of action program can be found at the Hyde Park Bank and Trust Company of Chicago. In this case the bank established an urban affairs department staffed with bankers, urban economists, and a sociologist. Here again Hyde Park has actually sought out potential black businessmen and tried to provide them with financial assistance. What makes the Hyde Park program so interesting is that the bank has established a special program to devote designated time and demand deposits to the maintenance of a loan fund for investment in inner-city projects, including economic development loans for minority businessmen. Of course, the bank's primary business is still the servicing of its large accounts, yet this technique is quite an unusual departure from conventional banking and its initial efforts appear to be highly successful.

Government Guarantees—Obviously, the high risk factor may still be present in efforts such as these. This is particularly true if a significant volume of inner-city loans is being considered. A tool commonly used to reduce this risk factor for a wide range of small business ventures has been the government (SBA) guaranty. While experimental efforts and programs to apply the guaranty to small scale minority business loans had been attempted with mixed results, it has only been since the summer of 1968 that, as Howard Samuels describes in chapter 5, it has been applied to larger scale minority business opportunities in a concentrated fashion. At that time the banking industry, through the American Bankers Association, and the Small Business Administration, under the leadership of Mr. Samuels, joined forces in a concentrated effort to provide increased opportunities for minority business development. Essentially, the program for increased minority entrepreneurship (dubbed "Project OWN" by SBA) provided for a national effort where banks would supply the capital and financial management assistance and SBA would provide a guaranty up to 90 per cent of the loan (maximum of $350,000). (See pages 70 and 72, *supra.*) This arrangement between the banks and SBA is not unlike other programs where the government acts as risk bearer for the private sector in order to achieve desired economic and social goals. Other primary features of the program include the provision of expert management assistance to the new entrepreneur through volunteer efforts of private industry, revised and liberalized credit criteria for such loans, utilization of community groups to identify capable business talent in the ghetto community and substantially reduced paperwork. As for results, while the track record is too short to evaluate successes and failures, in the first six months since the program was initiated the program's portfolio consisted of over 2,100 loans to minority businessmen valued at over fifty million dollars, with participation by a substantial number of the nation's commercial banks. Compared to past years' private and public lending schedules to minority businessmen, this joint effort stands out as an innovative device for "priming the pump" of credit to the depressed ghetto business sector.

Pooling Arrangements—One significant side effect of the increased social demand for capital from the ghetto communities as well as the impetus of individual bank initiatives throughout the country has been the formation of special purpose bank "pools" designed to increase credit flows to inner-city communities. Such pooling arrangements have taken various forms; some a loose federation where the banks agree to share risks for whatever capital needs arise, others a very formal arrangement separately administered, staffed and with specific dollar commitments of funds. Under the latter type, each bank may provide a certain amount of money to the pool based on its asset size, while the administration of the program may be centralized in one bank, may rotate from bank to bank, may be handled by the local clearing house or may rest with a newly created administering body. The advantage of a pooling arrangement is that it provides a broad forum for all banks in the community to participate, and as a result has the potential to generate a greater dollar volume of loan funds while reducing the risk factor which any one bank must bear. Variations of such pooling arrangements are currently in existence in Chicago, Houston, Trenton, Richmond, Philadelphia and other cities.

Continuing Problems

A mere examination of the dollar loan volume generated by these program efforts does not provide a true picture of the benefits and limitations involved. An objective evaluation can only be obtained by examining what transpires after the loans have been made—business profitability, jobs produced, dignity inspired—and by analyzing and remedying problems inherent in program administration. While results are quite mixed from community to community, they do give cause for limited optimism considering the magnitude of problems which must still be confronted and hopefully resolved.

MANAGEMENT ASSISTANCE

The relatively short experience we have clearly indicates that the availability and concentrated application of sound management experience and skilled professional assistance is essential to the viability of new business ventures in the ghetto community. The need for such assistance reflects a common need among the vast majority of new business ventures regardless of race, further aggravated by past exclusions of the black community from the capitalistic system which prevented the full development of a business tradition in that community. Several significant steps have been taken to marshall this type of assistance, but on a national basis the effort has been sporadic at best. For example, in many communities CPAs, lawyers, bankers and others are providing free aid in preparation of loan application forms and continue to provide follow-up services after the business becomes operative. Some companies are providing contracts on a special basis to insure product markets, and professional marketing men are helping the new businessmen learn effective ways to display, promote and sell their products and services. The possibilities of business success are markedly enhanced as a result of such assistance, but in many communities only a beginning has been made toward marshalling potential resource inputs of the private sector.

IDENTIFYING ENTREPRENEURS AND MARKETS

Two problems of identification are also prevalent. One involves the identification of entrepreneurial talent in the ghetto communities. Lacking the tradition of business experience, and given the prevailing distrust of the business community, solving this problem could be critical. Several approachs are being tried with varying degrees of success. Most attempt to utilize a local "screening" group from the community—community action groups, or a group of existing minority businessmen—while in some instances new organizations have been spawned to fill this role. The other area of identification involves that of markets, competition and long-range growth. Improper identification of market potential could lead quickly to business disaster, and this problem is compounded by present lack of operative economies in the ghetto communities. Accurate identification of both talent and markets is a major concern of today's committed businessmen, for they are apprehensive about the possibility of stimulating failure in the ghettos.

LOAN SERVICING COSTS

In addition, the administrative costs associated with such loans are apt to be quite high. Once the loan has been granted, it usually requires fairly close scrutiny to make sure the borrower uses the proceeds of the loan according to plan. Oftentimes the bank has to be alert for local business trends that could place the loan in jeopardy at some future point. In many cases the banks have initially done feasibility studies to examine the potential success of the minority entrepreneur's venture. All of these additional services require staff, time, and money and reduce the bank's margin of profit substantially.

LACK OF EQUITY CAPITAL

Furthermore, most of the minority lending programs attack only one dimension of the problem. In addition to working capital, the majority of these businesses require substantial injections of equity money. Since many of these businesses have been deficit operations in the past, the owner has had little opportunity to develop an equity base on which to request additional working capital. Also, it may be difficult to raise this type of money in the ghetto, since the residents often may not understand the nature of equity money, or given the week-to-week existence that is typical for many ghetto families, there may simply be no money to invest in such business ventures.

COMMUNITY UNDERSTANDING OF THE FINANCIAL SYSTEM

The final problem that must be overcome is communication with the ghetto concerning the impact of cyclical credit fluctuations. At the very time that the community becomes aware that conditions are improving and credit is being made available to potential entrepreneurs, credit could become tight during an inflationary market. What had first appeared as a favorable change then appears highly unfavorable, and the residents of the community again view the system as tending to choke off progress whenever the black man gets too close.

Another problem the bank may face is adverse community reaction to a foreclosure of the note on a locally owned business. Residents of the community may not understand the economics of an individual situation, and the bank's action may be interpreted as a racial act, even though its lending record in the minority community is a good one. It will often make little difference to certain members of the community that the business had no chance of success, and that the loan would have been foreclosed regardless of the man's color, race or name. A misunderstanding of such action can resurrect fears of the white man's money system holding the black man down "in his place." Under such pressures, bank officers can easily become hyperdefensive, and a cycle of mistrust and animosity can develop, thereby jeopardizing the success of legitimate efforts.

New Proposals

During the past year, additional solutions to the problems of credit flow to the ghetto community have been offered by public officials, major foundations, economic groups, civil rights organizations and others. Some of these proposals are extremely elaborate and would require significant changes in the economic structure of the inner cities. Others would make use of existing legislative devices and use large amounts of public funds to lever substantial private capital investment in the ghetto community. Still others would create new variations of tax incentives to induce private industry to use its capital and managerial expertise to develop the ghettos as economic entities. And finally, there are those who argue that only the public sector can marshal the necessary assets to achieve this face-lifting and, therefore, the federal government should oversee this task in its entirety.

COMMUNITY SELF-DETERMINATION ACT

Most complex of these proposals is the Community Self-Determination Act (the genesis of which is described in chapter 3 by Mr. McClaughry). This Act proposes to establish a complex system of development companies, community banks, and entrepreneurial operations within the confines of a specific geographical sector of the community. The legislation is based on the premise that only when the community has direct operating control over its economic institutions can real economic growth be achieved in accordance with community desires, and any other arrangement would make the community dependent on outside forces for its development.

While the goal of the Self-Determination Act explained in chapters 3 and 4—economic rebirth of the ghetto community—is laudable, a host of critics have attacked the proposal on philosophical, economic, and technical grounds. One primary objection goes to the heart of the legislation, claiming it is simply an attempt to establish separate black economic enclaves within the cities. An economic objection on the same issue questions the capability of ghetto communities to function as separate economic units, considering present diseconomies of such communities and the interrelated nature of our aggregate national, regional, and local economies.

The banking industry may view with great concern the proposed creation of a new community banking system on structural, functional and competitive grounds, particularly in light of the proposed incentive features provided to this new banking system. Others will argue that the methodology of the legislation imposes an unrealistic and inflexible bureaucratic framework on communities. Further, the legislation assumes by implication that a vast pool of talent exists to fill the numerous management and banking jobs required to operate this new community conglomerate structure. Finally, the political complexities of this legislation are overwhelming. It not only creates a forum for power struggles in the black community, but also implies a potential political confrontation between the black community and city hall, if only on the question of community services. And at a time when pressure for tax reform has reached significant proportions, and concern is evident over concentrations of economic power, this legislation takes a countervailing position on both points.

DOMESTIC "EDGE ACT" CORPORATIONS

With regard to the problem of equity capital, one recent proposal[1] recommends the establishment of domestic Edge Act corporations, which would provide a vehicle for commercial banks to assist indirectly in the equity financing of inner-city business development. With only limited exceptions, banks are presently precluded from direct equity investment in domestic corporations, while, since 1919, federal law[2] has provided the opportunity for stock ownership by banks in specially chartered corporations which can engage in equity financing of foreign businesses. While the holdings of these corporations are primarily in stock of financial enterprises, these corporations have made equity investments in a wide variety of non-financial businesses in foreign countries. Application of this concept domestically would enable banks to assist indirectly in the equity financing of those business enterprises necessary to improve the living conditions and economic development of our inner cities. Because of the high-risk nature of these investments, certain inducements—such as tax incentives or guaranteed debentures—may be essential to the effective organization of such corporations. The obvious and significant advantage of this approach would be to provide the ghetto with a substantial equity base.

OTHER EFFORTS TO PROVIDE EQUITY CAPITAL

A relatively limited number of programs are now in effect which address the problem. In both New York and Boston, pioneering efforts are being tested through the New York Urban Coalition's Venture Capital Corporation and Boston's Urban Foundation respectively. Both ventures raised substantial capital from private sector sources for reinvestment as equity capital in ghetto development enterprises, such capital being provided under liberal criteria and terms, and com-

[1] Brimmer, Andrew F., Member, Board of Governors of the Federal Reserve System, "The Banking System and Urban Economic Development," a paper presented to the 1968 Annual Meetings of the American Real Estate and Urban Economics Association and the American Finance Association, December 28, 1968.

[2] Section 25(a); 12 U.S.C. 611–631.

bined with sophisticated inputs of management consultation and support. Equity capital has also been raised successfully via the stock subscription route within the ghetto community itself, the most notable example being the Reverend Leon Sullivan's remarkable economic development program in Philadelphia, which, as Martin Skala describes in chapter 12, has provided required equity for a shopping center, apartment construction and the establishment of a community controlled aerospace company. Several other approaches are also being made through such devices as Small Business Investment Companies specifically designed to provide this type of investment capital, and at least one mutual fund with a limited percentage of its capital gains being earmarked for high risk ghetto investment.

Leveraging Public Deposits—Another proposal, now in actual operation in Illinois, is intended to link the use of public funds deposited in commercial banks with the achievement of certain social goals. In Illinois the State Treasurer has set aside a portion of state funds for just this purpose. He will then deposit an amount of these funds in those banks which make a commitment to invest a like amount in programs for low-income housing or minority business development. The Illinois State Treasurer feels the program has achieved a high degree of success, and proposals have now been made for a similar use of funds deposited in banks by the federal government and other state and local governments. (Further discussion of this "link deposit" device appears in chapter 10, by Dunbar McLaurin and Cyril Tyson.)

Tax Credits to Banks—Numerous additional techniques have been suggested to compensate commercial banks and other lending institutions for the extra risk they assume when lending in ghetto areas; however, many of these will require legislative changes at the national, state or local level. One such technique would be to allow banks and other commercial lenders an income tax credit against all business loans made in a ghetto area. This credit would be in addition to the normal bad debt allowance granted to banks. In effect, this system would increase the yield for the financial institution without forcing the borrower to assume higher credit costs.

Tax Credits to Industry—A variation in the same vein would be to provide tax credits to corporations which maintain deposits in commercial banks for the single purpose of making loans to ghetto entrepreneurs. For example, a corporation might receive a credit of four per cent of its average daily balance, or it could receive a credit against a portion of the interest its deposits would earn in time accounts. The leverage such a program would provide is extremely large. If, for example, 200 corporations each deposited $100,000 in such accounts, banks could provide credit to the ghetto in the amount of $20,000,000.

Assuming such deposits were placed in time accounts which paid an interest rate of five per cent, the total income earned by the corporations would be $1,000,000. If the government granted a credit of 20 per cent against such income, the government's revenue loss would be $200,000, in return for a generated investment of $20,000,000. A more limited version of this proposal, applying to tax credits for direct corporate investment in ghetto programs, is now underway in Pennsylvania.

Credit Development Corporations—Another possibility available to banks would be a credit development corporation, as was recently formed by Citizens and Southern National Bank in Georgia. Such corporations can be formed under present banking statutes and provide a unique source of funds for poverty communities. With an initial capitalization of $1,000,000, the newly formed Citizens and Southern Corporation is engaging in special high-risk situations which provide long-run economic benefits to the ghetto community, and, therefore, to the community at large. Presently the corporation is providing financing for second mortgages in the ghetto area and makes long-term "equity" loans to new and existing minority owned businesses. These corporations seem to provide an excellent opportunity for creative banking and this unique approach is sufficiently promising to warrant consideration by other banking institutions.

These, then, are some of the alternatives that could be used to increase the flow of credit to the ghetto economy. It is only a partial list, and certainly many more avenues need to be considered.

There is no doubt that American industry, including the banks, has spent far too little of its energies and financial resources to correct the inequities of the inner city. That tide is now turning. Bankers are proud that they helped build the cities of America. They have begun to recognize a responsibility to contribute positively to the revitalization of these same cities. A major goal of the Bankers Committee on Urban Affairs is to stimulate bank participation in the economic development of these cities, and their economically depressed communities in particular. The banking industry is moving toward positive, responsible action seeking sustained results.

David B. Hertz

8

Is Partnership Possible?

As the total stock
To the total gain or loss
So each man's particular stock
To his share of the gain or loss.

Encyclopaedia Britannica on
Partnership, 1st Edition, 1771

A true democracy cannot survive if any of its citizens are denied equal access to all of its rights, privileges, and substance. But the rules of the game in the United States over the last two centuries—both written and unwritten—have gradually forced a portion of our population into an immobile and static economic posture. The blacks in our central cities—numbering over 12 million, almost 40 per cent of whom live at or below a poverty income level [1]—are economically free in name only. And despite the changes made in our statutes and legal procedures thus far, these people do not really enjoy the rights and privileges guaranteed to all by our basic laws. Nor do they receive a fair share of our society's products.

Non-white unemployment in our inner cities is three times higher

---

DAVID B. HERTZ *is a director and senior partner of McKinsey and Company, Inc. A former president of the Institute of Management Sciences, Dr. Hertz has taught industrial engineering and operations research at Columbia University, conducted operations research at Arthur Andersen and Co., and written several articles and books, including* The Theory and Practice of Industrial Research.

[1] *Who are the Urban Poor?* by Anthony Downs, Committee for Economic Development, Supplementary Paper No. 26, October, 1968. (Data on employment and incomes are taken from this reference.)

than that of the metropolitan white population, but this unemployment rate seems to be only a reflection of a much more serious problem—that of closed opportunities and lack of upward mobility for those who do have jobs. Broad-based racial discrimination at all levels affects the marginally employable group; overt union discrimination and covert channeling of non-whites into dead-end jobs pervade the American economic structure.

Clifford L. Alexander, Jr., Chairman of the Equal Employment Opportunity Commission pointed clearly to this root problem when he said in the *Wall Street Journal,* January 15, 1968:

> It is a fairly well-known fact that a college-educated black man earns, at the median, less than a white high school dropout—barely two-thirds what a white man earns with a comparable level of education. What is less widely known . . . is that the disparity of income between black and white in America actually increases with the level of education attained. There is a closer approximation of equality in earnings among people with an elementary school education than there is among college graduates. . . .
>
> Even the companies who are determined simply to hire "a Negro" do not always succeed. They want a black man in order to put him in a special slot. Something like "director of Equal Opportunity Programs" is always a good one; there is just one to a company.

By any measure, our capital-rich and technology-loaded economy is pushing more and more of our underprivileged into an impossible economic position. It is true, of course, that in any highly industrialized environment, capital accumulation and technical progress raise the output per worker. However, the main influence on real wages in such an economy is not the average production of labor but rather the marginal product—the addition to the total national product arising from the employment of additional labor. Thus, in a highly technical society like the United States, since the marginal product is low, even though the average output per worker is high, wages paid will tend to become a decreasing proportion of total gross national product or income. The remainder of the GNP will go to the owners and managers of assets via profits, rents, and other shares in the return on capital.

In ghetto businesses, residents do not control the assets. Consequently, if industrial development leads to higher average outputs with a relative decline in the marginal product of the only major resource the ghetto has—labor, largely unskilled—the system will tilt more and more toward inequality of income distribution.[2]

Clearly, we must find solutions that will enable those encircled

[2] See J. E. Meade, *Efficiency, Equality, and the Ownership of Property,* Oxford, 1967.

and economically dominated areas we now call the ghettos to flourish. We must determine how to bring ghetto residents into the economic mainstream of American life. And we must ensure that their progress is adequate for their own needs and the country's.

While we can gradually change the historic factors and rules that have hedged these people in and created these ghettos, such changes will probably not accelerate the rate of economic progress enough to lift the ghettos out of their relative poverty, since the rest of the country will continue to move ahead on a fast track of affluence. Increasing the rate of economic progress is not, in any case, simply a matter of creating a few hundred thousand jobs; rather, it is a matter of finding a way to develop viable economic communities so that black businessmen, entrepreneurs, and institutional managers compete on an equal footing with their white counterparts in controlling available resources and so that these communities can contribute to the country's prosperity.

The Need for Indigenous Investment

The only resources the ghetto community really has are its human resources; consequently, its economic strength must rest on full utilization of these resources, of which there must be a self-feeding development. Specifically, investment mechanisms and economic tools must be carefully and subtly designed so that the disadvantaged communities will benefit at least triply from:

An increased volume of goods produced and services *available* on and by the home market to reduce the outflow of funds from the community;
The export of goods and services at higher values than at present, to raise the income level in the community; and
The retention of increasingly large shares of the profits and rents derived from capital used within the ghetto.

Simply providing short-term, incremental additions to the income of the black communities by additional low-paying jobs or by minor upgrading of entry-level pay scales will not accomplish these objectives. The ghetto resident's income is so low that this money will flow into the export stream and out of the ghetto almost immediately. And since he will have spent the additional income, no savings will accrue; and without savings there cannot be an effective asset shift. Thus, while living standards may rise slightly, the ghetto's economic structure will not significantly change. Only careful investment within the ghetto can ensure a reduction in cash outflows with an accompanying increase in ghetto-produced goods and services.

Consequently, efforts must be made to identify and finance those industries, businesses, and services that will make maximum use of the ghetto's human resources. And those enterprises must be designed to reduce the amount of imported goods and services and increase the value of ghetto exports (largely labor). Further, these enterprises must be job-creating, pride-building, and asset-shifting and must aim toward high marginal (labor) productivity.

However, blacks cannot develop these enterprises alone: the technical, managerial, and financial resources are simply not available. Neither can the white communities: attempts to impose solutions will not provide the needed growth of resources in the ghetto communities. So, if anything is to be accomplished, close working relationships in technical, managerial, and financial areas among black and white community leaders, entrepreneurs, and businessmen are essential. "The early years of TVA have also proved that the key to the entire process of democratic participation in the development process is the relationship created between the community and the people providing the service—managers, planners, technicians and so forth." [3]

The Importance of Co-existence

Despite any claims for separatism, there is no way in which any community can be completely isolated economically from all others. This would be true even if such an entity were extremely powerful. It is particularly true when that body is particularly weak in assets and other resources. Trade of some sort must exist between communities, but beyond weak one-sided trading relationships, there has to be a reciprocal flow of goods and services across boundaries where those goods and services are essential to the life and well-being of a community. For example, almost all ghetto economic enterprises will depend on public utilities, such as electric power. This would be true even if it were possible to turn these utilities back to the ghetto community since:

The investment in assets far exceeds any potential assets the black community could command;

The technical skills required to operate and manage such utilities are not now available within the community and are not likely to be for a long period of time; further, this technology will be changing and new investments will be needed; and

A large base of demand is necessary to make such enterprises viable. The ghetto alone cannot provide this base of demand.

These factors govern a host of enterprises and serve to indicate that, whatever economic, social, and political structures are established

[3] Arnold Schuchter, *White Power and Black Freedom,* Beacon Press, Boston, 1968; p. 207.

within the ghetto, there will still have to be a close and necessary cooperation with the white economic community. This relationship should influence, and to a certain extent determine, the serious development of entrepreneurship, asset ownership, and economic self-determination in the black communities. To be truly effective, this relationship should be a "partnership" freely entered into, with both sides having an equal voice in its formation and operation, open to withdrawal if either side does not satisfactorily engage in the spirit of the agreements reached. To achieve the proper balance between the vital white "cooperative" partnership component and the black "community based" partnership component will obviously be a difficult task. It should be perfectly clear that overwhelming economic strength lies on the cooperative side while the community essentially commands only its own moral and personal resources.

Just as there must be a cooperative partnership between communities, there should be at least initial partnerships between black and white ghetto endeavors if significant economic progress is to be made. Such partnerships can find ways to turn ghetto needs into ghetto assets:

> With no more investment than a phone call, these men can put a Negro in business, open a line of credit at a bank, or give him an order which . . . takes care of his credit and insurance problems—and these are what a black man trying to start just can't get. . . . it's almost a feudal system. All they (the white economic power structure) have to do is to move the smallest amount of muscle, and the city bounces.[4]

For example, the antiquated and massive bureaucracies of health and education as well as sanitation and protection might be supplanted by vigorous and effective local institutions utilizing ghetto labor at high marginal productivities. This could make a dent both in the export and import sides of the ghetto economic structure.

There is, however, no easy way—no panacea. It would be difficult to achieve these kinds of end results even in a sophisticated, resourceful, and rich community. "Asking many of today's institutions to respond to new needs is a little like putting a man on a windowsill and asking him to fly. Not only was he not built for flight but if you keep insisting he's likely to turn around and punch you in the nose." [5] The economic, social, and political obstacles to effective partnership are enormous. The white community's organizational, technical, and financial know-how must be harnessed in a viable—and possibly very

[4] Louis Winnick of The Ford Foundation, quoted in the *New York Magazine*, December 16, 1968.

[5] Richard Goodwin, "Sources of the Public Unhappiness," *New Yorker*, January 4, 1969.

long-term—relationship with the aspirations and requirements of the non-white community. Each side of the partnership must find a way to contribute what it must and take away what it must from the joint venture. Can it be done?

To answer this question, both communities will have to resolve many problems. Partnership—in any form—creates complex social, economic, and political problems. And when potential partners come to the table with different backgrounds, goals, and assumptions to deal with new, difficult, and potentially explosive issues, it will be particularly hard to achieve satisfactory working relationships.

With these objectives and problems in mind, what kind of picture can we piece together of partnership's role in the development of black capitalism? On the following pages I will attempt to answer that question.

Key Requirements

To be successful, any partnership must meet at least three requirements. And this is particularly true when the partners represent such diverse social and economic backgrounds. Specifically:

—there must be mutual understanding and trust between partners—they must be able to communicate with each other;
—each partner's role must be clearly defined; and
—the rules governing the partnership must be acceptabe to all.

MUTUAL UNDERSTANDING

Partnership, in the broadest sense, represents the most effective tool of the white entrepreneurial and managerial community. For partnership is a set of relations that exists between persons who carry out any activity together with a view of gain; and this gain need not necessarily be financial. The formal aspects of partnership, which we will come to later, require a legal reduction of this simple statement into a number of component parts. However, without this legal reduction, much of the economic structure of the white business world operates in partnership form. For example, the white businessman accepts as commonplace the ability to develop adequate agreements—whether written or not—among all interested parties[6] in a particular endeavor, but this ability to reach informal understandings becomes a key source of friction when black and white communities must work together. That is, when working out arrangements for any kind of economic enterprise, in which joint black and white managerial, tech-

[6] The entrepreneurs, the technicians, the capitalists, the suppliers of parts and services, the distributors, the labor components, regulatory and administrative agencies, the public, etc.

nical, and financial efforts are involved, the awareness that much of what is unspoken will ultimately be a part of the total endeavor—whether it is ever written down or not—is known clearly to one party and not to the other. Such "business" accommodations, working shorthands, communications devices, or unspoken agreements, are taught in the white community almost from birth. In the black community an entirely different communications structure has evolved and has been taught from birth. It has been based upon the necessity for codes and devices to deal effectively with the white man, by a special language and understanding in the community itself and in its transactions with the white world. Thus, questions of trust—whose word to believe and under what circumstances—constantly arise.

The trust that is necessary for successful negotiation in the ghetto is perhaps totally different from the kind of trust required by white businessmen. It is for these reasons, among others, that militant separatists feel that no dealings with the white community are possible.

DEFINING THE PARTNERS' ROLES

A partnership is, of course, a voluntary association and in general we cannot distinguish it from its members. Essentially, all the partners become agents of the partnership and, consequently, agents of the co-partners as well. However, the partners may agree to restrict the internal or external powers of any partner provided that notice is duly published to those who would do business with the partnership. Thus, if black and white communities are to enter into some form of partnership, the respective roles of the individuals involved must be clearly defined.

Generally, the white partners will bring to the enterprise the skills and technical competence that are indigenous to their business structure; the black partners must invest their energies, hopes, and communication skills to utilize effectively the assets of their white partners. The partnership as a whole of course will be liable for the acts of its partners and, ultimately, if each side has a clear expectation of what it may gain by the partnership, it may be possible to achieve some of the results we have been describing.

Perhaps most important of all is the requirement that partners provide each other with true accounts of all things affecting the relationship. Probably the greatest difficulty that has been encountered in the black-white relationship is that one side or the other feels it has not been kept fully informed. This is due partially to the lack of communication between the two parties. Consequently, much of what might go unsaid in either community needs to be said and explicitly spelled out between the two—and even then there is the chance of continued misunderstanding. Therefore, the partnership's aims, objectives, and rules probably need to be repeated over and over again. Nor should the participants be allowed to forget that in any partnership, patience is the secret ingredient for success.

THE RULES OF PARTNERSHIP

There must also be clear-cut understanding among the partners concerning the rules by which their business will be conducted. The partners may, in the normal course of affairs, agree to whatever rules they wish to follow. However, it has proved exceedingly difficult in white-black business relationships to reach an understanding on what these rules may be. Such rules must include how to admit new partners and how to make decisions within the new enterprise.

A key element in the agreement must be how the partnership is to be dissolved. If the objective of the partnership is to develop viable ghetto enterprises, ultimately these businesses should be wholly controlled by partners within the black community. And although some continuing relationship with the white partners may be desirable, the actual formal relationship should eventually be dissolved. (We have noted already that there are many informal partnership relationships in the white community. We would anticipate that such would be the case for these successful ghetto enterprises.)

Finally, to ensure the success of business partnerships between whites and blacks, certain key factors must be considered. First, the nation's financial resources must be tapped to cover initial costs. For example, the investment required to create one meaningful job is estimated to be about $10,000. Additionally, to train an unskilled worker would add another $5,000 of initial cost.

Second, innovation is essential. New kinds of community-based and -managed investment can add significantly to the income of communities and lessen the exportation of earnings.

Third, the disparity between black and white earnings must be reduced. Increasing earnings through capital investment, retraining, and other means will generate additional income, some of which will stay within the community. But inevitably a large part of these earnings will still flow to increase the Gross National Product and the return on the total national investment in productive resources.

Fourth, the white community's technical resources and managerial skills are neccessary if ghetto economic development is to be successful. Without this input the communities will not be able to pull themselves up by their own economic bootstraps and generate directly and indirectly a changed economic, social, and political climate.

In summary then, to provide ghetto residents equal opportunity, the partnership must be a bridge, a gap-closing device, a mechanism with adequate rules and communications that will train people, tap resources to develop communities and enterprises, and initiate changes in political, social and economic structures.

What Has Been Done

Specific efforts have already been made through:

The Office of Economic Opportunity's community action program;
The Economic Development Administration (EDA) Program in Oakland, California;
Other partnership efforts on the part of private businesses; and
The Bedford-Stuyvesant project.

OEO Community Participation Act

Attempts have been made to bring the white community—both the public and private sectors—into some kind of effective relationship with the non-white ghettos. The OEO Community Participation Act of a few years ago was designed to create a program:

Which mobilized and utilized resources, public or private . . . in an attack on poverty;
Which provided services, assistance and other activities . . . to give promise of progress toward elimination of poverty or a cause or causes of poverty through developing employment opportunities, improving human performance, motivation, and productivity, or bettering the conditions under which people live, learn, and work;
Which developed, continued, and administered with the maximum feasible participation of residents of the areas and members of the groups served; and
Which is conducted, administered, or coordinated by a public or private non-profit agency. . . .[7]

This statement of participation was a clear call to partnership, and from the beginning, many OEO members took it very seriously.

But community reaction to this program was apparently more than most politicians bargained for: i.e., the communities began to take hold of the political process. Ultimately the politicians were unable to accept this kind of social experimentation, and few effective results were achieved. The lesson was learned that once the community felt it had a role in the control of its own affairs, it moved not simply in economic directions but in political and social ones as well. And by the end of 1966, OEO had begun to cut back on its community action program.[8]

[7] Section 202A, Title II, Economic Opportunity Act of 1964.
[8] John C. Donovan, *The Politics of Poverty,* Pegasus, New York, 1967.

THE EDA PROGRAM

In 1966 in Oakland, California, Eugene Foley, then Director of the Economic Development Administration, Department of Commerce, conducted a major experiment in the use of federal funds to provide jobs and training for the unemployed in the Oakland ghettos. This project was put under the direction of Amory Bradford. At that time, the forces of order and stability in the white economic community were locked in a battle with the ghetto leaders. Consequently, this economic development and administration project was to establish a direct relationship among state, local, and federal programs, and was to develop a basis for increased respect among businessmen, labor leaders, and the ghetto residents.

The Economic Development Administration committed almost $30 million to Oakland. These funds provided a significant start in meeting the need for jobs and new businesses. However, each of the proposed projects—e.g., World Airways' plans for a new hanger at Oakland airport and a program for training aircraft mechanics (a $10 million investment on the part of EDA) ; Bennie's Candies ($55,000) ; Rainbow Carwash ($135,000); Colombo Bakers ($423,000)—caused a great deal of turmoil in the form of conflicting goals and competition for jobs and funds. These projects also demanded a tremendous amount of time on the part of all concerned and, in the end, served only to indicate how deep and permanent a commitment to the idea of partnership must be if success of this kind is to be achieved.[9]

Foley says, following the work of the EDA in Oakland, "We need bold and imaginative action in each ghetto and we offer inducements to obtain it. If we can devise schemes for a legitimate profit to be made in the ghetto then we will see the vast economic and talent resources of American business begin to apply themselves to the solution of urban problems." [10]

OTHER PARTNERSHIP EFFORTS

There are many kinds of cooperative black/white business experiments being attempted at the present time. The F. W. Woolworth Co. and the Equitable Life Assurance Society recently sold a major $2 million Woolworth property in Harlem to Harlem Freedom Associates, a newly-formed, limited partnership composed of Harlem community citizens. Ultimately, the land will be held in trusteeship for the Harlem community. The partnership will lease the store back to Woolworth.

[9] Amory Bradford, *Oakland's Not for Burning* (New York: David McKay Company, Inc., New York, 1968).

[10] Eugene P. Foley, *The Achieving Ghetto* (Washington, D.C.: The National Press, Inc., 1968).

Clarence Jones, a black officer of Carter, Berlind & Weill, the white investment house that worked out this transaction, described it as "land reform":

> For a generation, our leaders have preached to underdeveloped nations that they must reform the concept of land ownership and use so as to hold the political loyalty of their people. Yet we have ignored that same basic problem in the underdeveloped areas of the United States. The "Woolworth project" shows what can be done. However, the control of the economic enterprise which uses the land remains outside the black community.

Action Industries, Inc., a ghetto conglomerate, was formed in Venice, California. The white community surrounding the ghetto contributed both advice and financial support. The project was capitalized by a $1 million stock sale. All 500,000 shares of Class B common stock were restricted to a non-profit organization, Project Action, to insure community control of the company. Most of the company's directors will be elected by Project Action and will, therefore, be black residents of Venice.

The Watts ghetto is the site of at least two examples of successful partnership. One is the Green Power Foundation (90 per cent of the charter members are black businessmen and engineers), whose first project is the California Golden Oaks Products Co., a baseball-bat manufacturer. A $50,000 loan from the local telephone company and 18 other firms has already been repaid. The second example is the Watts Manufacturing Co., an Aerojet-General subsidiary largely managed and staffed by Watts residents. Martin Skala describes it in chapter 12.

A group of black and white businessmen in Portland, Oregon, established the Albina Corp., which manufactures fiberglass products—mainly boats. Employees of this company, who are largely local residents, hold the company stock.

In Washington, D.C., a black-managed and operated woodworking company was formed under the auspices of the Martin Marietta Corp., the federal government, and a small group of black residents. And the Greater Detroit Board of Commerce established an "Adopt a Business" program, under which a successful firm "adopts" a black-owned company and provides the guidance necessary for success.

The R.B.O.C. (Rochester Business Opportunities Corp.), also described in chapter 12 by Mr. Skala, is an effort by major businesses in Rochester, New York, to provide technical assistance to black enterprises.

Harlemdata, an EDP service bureau, has been established by a group of Harlem community leaders. It is specifically oriented to handling the needs of pharmacists and medical professionals who deal with the city administration under Medicare and Medicaid. The white business community's part in these efforts consisted of providing both managerial and technical (legal and financial) assistance, and white individuals have become limited partners in the enterprise. The city has worked with the partnership to develop improved service mechanisms that ultimately may apply to a large number of ghetto communities. From the beginning, the community group led the way in choosing its own goals and objectives and the whites who were involved provided the structure and mechanisms for achieving these goals.

The black and white communities are clearly involved in the process of learning to work together. The National Urban Coalition has been attempting to develop and foster genuine partnerships among community members, businessmen, labor and church leaders in cities throughout the country. The New York Urban Coalition is an example of what can be done in a genuine partnership arrangement. The black and Puerto Rican members of the Coalition, as a group, must approve any significant action or policy, whether taken by the Board of the Coalition (on which they are fully represented) or the executive staff. A genuine dialogue is in the process of development, and in the case of certain subsidiaries[11] of the Coalition, agreement has been reached to increase year-by-year community participation until these subsidiaries are fully community owned and controlled. Much has been done, but "much" is too little and too late. Further, a great deal has been done with a lack of adequate understanding on both sides.

THE BEDFORD-STUYVESANT PROJECT

The Robert F. Kennedy program for Bedford-Stuyvesant, a Brooklyn community of 450,000 people, was a sophisticated political attempt to change the economy and ecology of one of the nation's worst ghettos. A partnership of politicians, key businessmen, and some representatives of the black community has through the Bedford-Stuyvesant Restoration Corporation and the Bedford-Stuyvesant Development Services Corporation, managed to produce mortgages for area housing, establish some new plants (e.g., IBM is spending $300,000 to create 300 jobs in a cable plant), finance a number of small businesses, and train several hundred hard-core unemployed.

However, despite its success, the Bedford-Stuyvesant project has come up against significant obstacles. Specifically:

> The white business community (the board of the Bedford-Stuyvesant Development Services Corporation is all white) is not directly involved in the activities of the Bedford-Stuyvesant Restoration Corporation;

[11] Specifically, the Coalition Venture Corporation, a venture capital subsidiary, that has the charge of using Coalition and other funds to make seed-money loans for economic development purposes in New York ghettos.

Political pressures force individual politicians to fragment the end results in the community itself, rather than attempt to coalesce them;
There is no satisfactory white technical support responsive to the needs of the black staff personnel; and
Financial input is inadequate.

These obstacles have prevented what might have been a great example of partnership from being little more than another inadequate attempt to solve the ghetto problem.

Is Partnership Possible?

Both the successes and the inadequacies of the existing or past partnership attempts raise questions about the future of the black/white partnership concept.

1. *Is the white community prepared to provide the time necessary to meet the commitment of an operationally effective partnership?* The very people in the white community who could do this are the ones who are most engaged elsewhere. Is it always necessary that the well-meaning but less competent represent the white community?
2. *Are there enough trained people in the non-white communities to carry the heavy burden of a difficult partnership?* Lack of time, experience, and background creates frustration. And frustration is hardly the characteristic of a good partnership.
3. *Can the two communities learn to communicate with each other?* In almost every partnership to date, there has been a breakdown or an incipient breakdown in communications between key participants. For this, among other reasons, black separatists are attempting to exclude whites from their affairs.
4. *Can the white financial, legal, industrial, business and political communities commit themselves significantly to anything other than prestigious, image-building projects?* We have already seen how projects face several obstacles to success because the needed white technical support is not available. And the white personnel who do commit themselves may not be those with the highest fund of skill and capabilities.
5. *Is the black community ready to provide the* quid pro quo *in terms of ego or other satisfactions necessary to damp the impatience of the white power structure for immediate action-oriented projects and publicity-directed results?* The psychology of partnership calls for some kind of gain for both sides. And despite the view that profits will lure white resources into the ghetto, key resources will probably not move without other rewards. These must come from the blacks themselves. To play on the fears and guilt of those whites so afflicted will neither attract nor maintain the kinds of constructive partnerships essential for progress.
6. *Are the goals of the potential partners sufficiently congruent to make an effective partnership possible?* Many of the non-white middle class

> have aspirations similar to those of the white middle class and they, of course, should be able to work together. But, the black middle class groups are also striving for a sense of prideful self-identity and may not be ready to simply accept these aspirations as adequate or desirable. And what of the goals of the militants, those who do not necessarily wish to share in the precise end objectives of the majority of whites?

These are the chief questions that remain to be answered in considering the possibility of partnership between the two communities. However, no matter how they are answered, what will have to be done is clear: the circle of poverty, low pay, inadequate educational facilities, poor community services, and no power in the economic world must be broken. Massive aid programs are not enough, and community self-help will not do it. As Kenneth Clark told the Kerner Commission: "Business and industry are our last hope. They are the most realistic elements of our society. Other areas in our society—government, education, churches, labor—have defaulted in dealing with Negro problems." [12]

And, according to Gar Alperovitz, "We are entering the age of advanced technology . . . and we need the sophistication of the large corporations. We can't do without them." [13]

Partnership, with all its difficulties, may be the only practical solution. But flexibility and imagination will be demanded of both black and white if such partnerships are to develop the philosophy, organization, and administrative methodology that will permit the world in which the partners must live to survive.

[12] Quoted in *New York Magazine,* December 16, 1968, p. 34.
[13] Gar Alperovitz in *New Generations,* Fall 1968, p. 26.

Lawrence Johnson and
Wendell Smith

9

Black Managers

As the decade of the 1960s drew to a close, the curtain began to rise on a new chapter in the black businessman's fight for economic inclusion, or, in President Nixon's words, "a piece of the action."

The Dismal Past

In the past, Negro business efforts have been very limited, both in number and in scope. Until comparatively recently, the Negroes' lack of business experience and management skills, shortage of financial resources, and inability to raise capital or to rent space all combined to cause them to downgrade commercial enterprise. Entry into the professions was stressed, instead.

Negro businesses that did develop have generally been confined to small operations in racially restricted markets where segregation provided a "crutch." They were mainly single proprietorships—many of them requiring the pooling of family labor to make them going

---

LAWRENCE A. JOHNSON *is assistant dean in the School of Business Administration at the University of Massachusetts. Dean Johnson has taught at Arkansas AM & N College, North Carolina College and San Francisco State. He is a contributing author to the study* The U.S. Negro *and author of "Hiring the Hard Core Unemployed." He is a consultant to government and industry in the area of minority employment.*

WENDELL R. SMITH *is dean of the School of Business Administration at the University of Massachusetts. Dr. Smith has taught marketing at the University of Iowa and the Wharton School of Finance and Commerce of the University of Pennsylvania. A former staff vice president of the Radio Corporation of America, Dean Smith is a past president of the American Marketing Association.*

concerns—and were heavily concentrated in services to which free access was denied to Negro consumers elsewhere. Most common were beauty and barber shops, luncheonettes and restaurants, funeral parlors, and hotels. Negroes shied away from enterprises in which the Negro consumer's dollar found ready acceptance in the open market, such as department stores, hardware, furniture stores, and similar outlets. There are few Negro manufacturing firms, because considerable capital and the existence of broad markets are requirements not easily met. The few enterprises that did develop were predominantly devoted to beauty products. The implications of this situation were unfortunate. Non-white communities are in great need of prosperous small businessmen. Aside from the fact that they are in a position to offer employment to members of their own ethnic group, it is believed by many that successful entrepreneurs usually contribute leadership, stability, and continuity to a neighborhood.

BANKING AND LIFE INSURANCE

The few attempts to develop large businesses were also restricted to areas where the competition had no desire to enter. It was not until the turn of the century that non-whites were able to buy coverage from national life insurance companies, and even then they were often forced to pay higher premiums. This spurred the development of some black controlled insurance companies. In 1962 there existed about fifty such companies but they were playing a very limited role in the writing of insurance even for black policyholders. The largest company of this type had total assets of about $77 million, and the twenty leading companies had combined assets that amounted to about $300 million, a minimal share of the more than $30 billion total for the insurance industry.

In banking the record was even more dismal. In 1963 there were only 13 black banks in the country. There has been some expansion since 1963; five new banks were chartered by the end of 1964 and since then many small black banks have been emerging across the country. It was not until 1965 that Harlem's first black-chartered and black-operated commercial bank was opened. Appropriately named the Freedom National Bank, it has been growing fast, although five United States banking giants still maintain branch offices in the area.

The history of black business can only be classified as insignificant in the total picture. Even this marginal participation has been declining as a percentage of the total.

In the decade between 1950 and 1960 the number of self-employed Negro businessmen was reduced by more than 20 per cent (see chart on page 115), largely as the result of competition by stronger white-owned firms. The greatest decline occurred in transportation, where marginal small-scale Negro operators had to bow to large truck and taxi fleet owners. Some Negro firms in communications, utilities, and sanitary services also succumbed.

The Way to the Future

The three major barriers to entry into business for black entrepreneurs have been: (1) inability to raise the capital needed, (2) the attitudes of the buying public, both black and white, toward the black businessman and (3) the lack of management skills.

CAPITAL

Lending institutions have in the past almost completely ignored the opportunities offered by investing in business owned by blacks. In the few instances when such investments were made, they tended to be small and normally carried with them higher rates of interest. This coolness on the part of lending institutions could perhaps be traced to the fear of failure of the black business and hence the loss of investment. Part of the refusal to lend is attributable to the lack of assets held by borrowers needed to protect such loans. This inability to find funds in order to build assets locks the small businessman into a vicious circle. Efforts by the federal government to protect lending institutions against loss free some capital for the black community. Even with this protection, not many risks are being taken by the non-white lending institutions. Banks are held responsible by the government for checking the risk factor. In such cases, banks can recover from the government in the event of failure, but they remain cautious in their lending to avoid establishing a high failure record with the federal agency. Church groups and some charitable organizations are making more risk capital available to the black community through black banks. Competition from these black-owned banks serves as an inducement to the liberalization of credit on the part of white lending institutions.

ATTITUDES OF THE BUYING PUBLIC

Success in any business endeavor requires that the public being served provide continued support by purchasing the goods or services offered. Such support is usually given because of the value of the services that are offered. It is often withheld for poor service or poor value. It can also be withheld if the seller is forced to compete with others who may have the advantage of being members of the same ethnic group, or in many instances, of having the same color skin as the buying public. Black businessmen have had to "pay a tax" in this type of environment in that few could enter and sell successfully in the broad market. At

Self-Employed Negro Businessmen, 1950 and 1960

Industry	1950		1960		Annual % Rate of Change 1950–1960
	Total Negro	Negro as % of Total	Total Negro	Negro as % of Total	Negro
Construction	3,390	1.7	3,978	1.8	1.6
Manufacturing	1,050	0.4	1,376	0.8	2.7
Transportation	2,430	4.7	1,241	3.2	−6.5
Communications, utilities & sanitary services	270	6.3	82	1.7	−11.2
Wholesale trade	2,640	1.5	2,610	1.9	−0.1
Retail trade	38,730	2.8	26,303	2.6	−3.8
Food & dairy prods.	14,520	3.9	8,740	4.1	−4.9
Eating & drinking places	15,030	5.5	11,344	5.6	−2.9
Genl. mdse. & ltd. price variety	750	1.2	640	1 3	−1.6
Apparel & accessories	600	0.7	321	0.6	−5.9
Furniture & homefngs.	360	0.5	182	0.4	−6.1
Motor vhcls. & access.	180	0.3	163	0.3	−0.9
Gas service stations	1,290	0.9	2,153	1.4	5.3
Hardware, bldg. materials	120	0.2	80	0.1	−3.9
Other retail trade	5,880	2.8	2,680	1.8	−7.5
Banking and finance	90	0.4	41	0.2	−7.5
Insurance & real estate	600	1.3	794	1.6	2.8
Business services	570	1.7	890	2.4	4.6
Auto. repair & garages	870	1.5	1,083	2.8	2.2
Misc. repair services	450	1.5	414	2.1	−0.8
Personal services	5,970	4.4	4,349	3.4	−3.1
Other industries	2,760	2.8	3,239	3.4	1.6
Total	59,820	2.5	46,400	2.4	−2.4

Source: The American Negro Reference Book, p. 292.

one time the barbershop services, particularly in the south, were almost exclusively black. Competition from whites soon began to eat away at this monopoly and today it is rare that one can find black barbers operating in white communities, north or south.

The other side of the coin is just as cruel in that black customers tended to deal with black businessmen only if the circumstances forced such dealings. The very fact that most ghetto stores were white owned and operated is evidence of this fact. In some instances the problem was not a lack of capital. Blacks do own and operate beauty shops, barber shops, etc., in the ghetto, but where black buyers had a choice they chose the white owned and operated stores. Such behavior must be attributed to a lack of confidence in the black businessman. Success in business is necessary in order to build confidence. Sales are essential to success. Here again the black businessman is locked into a circle of failure.

Capital is now being made available to non-white businessmen through many channels. The new mood of black people sweeping the country will erase the attitudes held by black buyers toward black businessmen. But as this mood gathers momentum, the consumers will begin to demand that they receive goods and services that are competitive. The possession of a black skin will not in itself be reason to expect the patronage of black customers. The black entrepreneurs will have to compete. This means the businessmen will have to possess certain business skills.

MANAGERIAL SKILLS

The new emphasis from the black community will surely enhance the opportunities for black businessmen to be successful in small businesses. Beyond the usual types of businesses that in the past were black owned and operated, there lie many opportunities. The development of franchising has opened many doors. Small manufacturing plants are possibilities, retailing to a larger market and in previously unprofitable fields is also open. Aside from the many opportunities offered the entrepreneur, industry's needs will require black managers to work in ghetto-based plants and elsewhere. A growing number of firms are returning to the core city and erecting plants within the ghetto. Some of these new efforts, described in chapter 12 by Martin Skala, have been attacked as outside colonial economic control. We feel that, granted white ownership in a transitional stage, these plants will eventually have to be managed by blacks if they expect to remain in the ghetto.

Opportunities to work in industry, in plants outside the ghetto, also exist. Most major companies now include visits to the predominantly black campuses in their recruiting schedules. The demand for black managers, whether it be for small business or to fill positions of responsibility in a major firm, in fact far exceeds the supply. Black capitalism as a concept can only come to fruition if black managers in significant numbers can be trained.

Any approach to the training of black managers must be made with the understanding that there is no formula that can produce an "instant" manager, black or white. The process is not too clearly understood by the many people involved in such training and perhaps even less understood among the people being trained.

The need to do this training and development job immediately requires that different approaches be made to each segment of the problem. The small entrepreneur, the manager of a ghetto-based enterprise, and the manager operating within the framework of a major corporation will require programs designed to train each to do a different type of job.

The term "management" is a many-sided thing with so many meanings that it sometimes appears to be meaningless. We often speak of the "management of the ABC Corporation." It is sometimes used to describe a specific kind of activity, e.g., "a marketing manager." On other occasions we speak of the "management team," and this term seems to incorporate everyone who wears a white shirt or has an office of a certain size. Basically, the process of managing boils down to:

Establishing objectives;
Directing others in the attainment of these objectives; and
Measuring the results.

These steps are the basic components of every manager's job, from the firm's president, who has an overall responsibility, down to an office manager whose jurisdiction may encompass only a few people. They also represent the steps that an entrepreneur operating his own business must follow if he is to be successful.

Black-Owned Businesses

Many Americans, black and white, thrive on Horatio Alger myths and are hard put to imagine how it is that one's own resources can be insufficient to conquer the myriad and complex problems of operating a business. This belief persists in an environment that is recording the steady decline of small businesses: During recent years about 300,000 businesses in the United States have discontinued each year according to the Small Business Administration.

The greatest hurdle that small businessmen have to overcome is the belief that one enters business and succeeds merely because he is willing to open a store and work hard. The flood of black people setting up businesses today is testimony to the fact that this belief is still very strong in the black community.

To a large extent black people have been excluded from the world of business, not merely because they were black but because they have not been able to assemble whatever mixture of variables it takes to become a successful businessman. Little is known about these variables. A strong desire for money, more than one might earn working for others, appears to be one basic motive. The need for independence is often quoted as another. But in addition to these motives one needs certain other characteristics. A high degree of tenacity is needed in order to weather the rough periods that will surely come. These motives and characteristics are surely not the sole possession of any one ethnic group. They are human traits possessed by people black and white.

A strong external force that contributes to the making of a successful businessman is the model or example one seeks to emulate. Examples play a major role in attracting people to certain occupations. Images of success serve not only as a model for action, but also as psychological supports for the probability of "making it." Such examples are rare in black America. In white America, often within the ring of friends and relatives, there exist examples of business success in abundance. Radio, movies, and television reinforce this success image. These examples lend a degree of credibility to the belief that one can succeed in business. The family, relatives, or friends also serve as sources of advice, finance, contact, or even offer a place where one can serve out an internship while learning. Such resources have been unavailable to black people attempting to enter the world of business. Yet, perhaps more than any other set of variables, these are really the external keys to success:

1. The ability to learn a business without taking a high capital risk;
2. The opportunity to seek advice from someone who has had experience;
3. The ability to borrow money without the necessity of becoming an instant success in order to feed one's family or to start the repayment of a loan; and
4. The ability to face friendly markets that will trade with you if your goods or services are competitive.

The ghetto entrepreneur may still be restricted to the kinds of businesses that were operated by white merchants who left the ghetto because of community pressures. Such retail businesses were usually successful because they operated when larger stores were closed, or they offered conveniences such as location or credit. The inability to compete with the established units of large chain systems caused most of these operations to charge higher prices, though surely some charged higher prices merely because the merchants could exploit the ignorance of the customer.

Some blacks view with suspicion the new breed of entrepreneurs and warn that the residents of the ghetto are not interested in merely changing exploiters. This puts even more pressure on the new entrepreneur in that he may be viewed with suspicion and is expected to operate his business quite differently from his predecessor.

TRAINING

The training of managers at whatever level is not a simple matter. It is certainly not something that can be done "instantly," and yet the demand for managers to operate ghetto enterprises is overwhelming.

If this new entrepreneur is to survive and find success he will need the constant support of knowledgeable business people. This support cannot operate on a once-a-week basis but must be available daily. It must be involved in the most minute aspects of the business while the owners learn. It is not something that can be taken into the classroom. (Time does not permit.) But it must take place in his daily operation. Such involvement has been undertaken by some schools of business located in major cities across the country.

An example is the Business Assistance Program (BAP), started in the fall of 1966 by a group of Harvard MBA candidates. BAP was underwritten by a three-year grant from The Ford Foundation, and is designed as a consulting service to help black entrepreneurs of small businesses introduce sound, modern, and rational methods into their operations. An underlying premise of the founders was that an economically strong black community (or that of any other ethnic group) would improve its relationship with society both economically and socially. In the first year, eight two-men teams were active as consultants to the businessmen in the community, and the number of clients has increased steadily. The program is entirely a student venture, neither supported nor controlled by the school. At the request of the students, however, members of the faculty have served as advisors. In most instances, the student-consultants (who are paid at the rate of $2.00 an hour from Ford Foundation funds to provide incentive and to avert the sense of charity) have provided guidance in such areas as bookkeeping, merchandising, credit policy, or making application for Small Business Administration loans.

The program is affiliated with two local Negro groups: Jobs Clearing House and Opportunities Industrialization Center. Both have provided the students with advice and direction in approaching the black community. The students are also working with such organizations as the NAACP and SNAP (South End Neighborhood Action Program).

The response from the black business community has been quite positive.

Other schools of business throughout the country are also involved in this type of help. Many operate without the benefit of outside funds, participating solely on a voluntary basis. One such program is conducted at Stanford University where the students work with small businessmen in San Francisco as well as the Bay area. Northeastern University conducts seminars for businessmen in the Roxbury community, and there are programs at Columbia and New York University.

Most of these programs are assisting businessmen who are already involved in business. They attempt to identify the errors that might otherwise have been made and to turn the operation into a profitable one. A greater need exists at the time of launching a business, when such programs could increase the probability of success. The programs should include the following items:

a. An accurate means of appraising entrepreneurial potential. Such a technique would be helpful for the black or white aspirant. It would allow selection of individuals with a high degree of potential and reduce the rate of failure.
b. An honest look at the enterprise the individual desires to undertake, which would help assure the existence of a market before the investment of time and money is made. This type of research is seldom done —perhaps the one single omission most responsible for small business failures. (Small businessmen, regardless of color, seem to enter fields where others appear to be doing well and assume theirs will be a like fate. Such reasoning is often just an open invitation to disaster.)
c. Formalized training in the rudiments of running a business. This is an undertaking that a university could handle. It requires the development of a special curriculum designed to meet the immediate needs of the businessmen. Such an undertaking on the part of a university could fit into the "total system" of an urban studies program, if one exists on the campus.
d. Consultants to work with individuals in their day-to-day operation. This is perhaps the greatest need, especially in the early stages when decisions have to be made that could affect the future of the business.

If these steps could be implemented, the probability of success would be increased and the creation of a class of black entrepreneurs would be hastened.

Managing the Ghetto Based Plant

The ideal manager for a ghetto based plant of a major company must be black, college trained, possessing the latest business tools and having served an apprenticeship in several slots within the corporate family. Such people, if they exist at all, are very rare indeed.

For too long blacks have been excluded from meaningful jobs in the world of business. This exclusion has led black students away from business and into such fields as education, social work, medicine, dentistry, law, and the ministry. In the predominantly white schools of business today few black faces will be found. The predominantly black colleges of this country are not providing the business tools that permit young people to equip themselves for advanced study in the field of business or for entry into business with the skills needed to succeed and advance. Only one undergraduate school, Texas Southern, is an accredited member of the American Association of Collegiate Schools of Business. The Graduate School of Business at Atlanta University is in the process of seeking membership, which will make it the first black graduate school with accreditation. Atlanta University is the only black school in the country with a graduate school of business. What is needed immediately is a supply of competent black managers to fill the many jobs that are available and will become available in the near future.

Managers for these jobs will differ significantly from the small entrepreneur. Formal training will be a necessity and may even require work beyond the undergraduate degree. If these plants are to be treated as independent profit centers it will be necessary to train other people in special areas such as accounting, marketing, and finance, to support the manager. Many firms attempt to solve this delicate problem by placing a black in training in the ghetto plant with a trained white from within the corporate family to actually run the plant while the black learns the ropes. Learning the ropes under these circumstances is difficult at best, and the results are usually very unsatisfactory. What is needed is an accelerated program that will measure the new manager's weaknesses as they relate to the task he will be performing, and then to design a program that will permit him to gain these needed skills. On-the-job support from the corporate headquarters will be needed in order to protect him in decision-making areas until he has gained the needed experience. Such experience is usually gained by serving some time under a senior person within the firm. In this case the time fuse is much too short and the demand is too great.

The acquisition of these skills can be brought about in many ways, some efficient and many costly and inefficient. As noted, some companies attempt to conduct what amounts to an on-the-job training program for their future black managers. This technique has the built-in problem of not really permitting the new manager to manage, not really allowing him to have the authority or the responsibility and, hence, to gain the respect of his work force. The presence of a white "support" says quite clearly to the rest of the workers who is really in charge.

Another problem associated with such a technique is the difficult question of when to release the manager and let him swim. Other firms employ the strategy of allowing their workers to gain the needed skills in evening programs conducted by the local college or university. These programs do serve a purpose, but where the aim is to create competent managers quickly, this avenue is neither fast nor efficient. The dropout rate from evening programs tends to be quite high.

Many companies have created their own programs, some going so far as to construct campus-like sites for this endeavor. Of the three techniques mentioned, this may be the most efficient for the rapid training of a ghetto plant manager. Such a program permits the company to design the material to fit the immediate needs of the trainee. It also permits the firm to place him on the job in a shorter period of time, allowing him to continue the formal side of the training while actually performing as a manager. Because of the time constraint, this manager will still lack the in-depth training needed to become a truly effective executive. Continued exposure to new problems and new techniques, should, over a period of time, help correct this deficiency. Many companies participate in university run programs designed to bring executives up-to-date in their respective areas. Attendance at sessions of this type, after a firm base has been established, will permit this "new" black manager to become even more effective.

THE BLACK EXECUTIVE

Few firms recruited at predominantly black campuses until quite recently. Now most of the major firms include these campuses in their recruitment schedule. It has been estimated that between 1964 and 1965, approximately 5000 graduates of these schools have been hired by industry. The accelerated hiring of these young men and women by the leading companies will be only a temporary palliative unless they can compete effectively for promotion. The lack of accreditation and the de-emphasizing of business in most of the curricula leave the majority of these young people ill-equipped to function effectively above the entry-level type job. According to the United States Department of Health, Education, and Welfare, only 116 of the 1966 graduates from the 82 predominantly Negro four-year colleges and universities majored in accounting. Many of the schools lack departments in the area of marketing, finance, or management. A lack of faculty depth compounds the problem. A side effect is the current raiding by industry of the few black faculty available to teach in the area of business.

It is difficult if not impossible for most of these young men and women to be effective above the entry-level type job. They soon find out that a real "educational gap" exists between them and their white fellow aspirants also seeking more responsibility.

To a degree, this problem can be minimized by company supported evening courses. However, if some of the more sophisticated and computer-oriented techniques are to be mastered, a concentrated, full-time program will be required. Lately, schools of business have become actively involved in the task of designing programs to prepare black students for management positions. These programs are few in number at the moment but new ones are constantly being established. The programs differ in approach but the end objectives are the same: to create a pool of competent managers as quickly as possible.

Five schools[1] formed a consortium to tackle the problem at one level. The consortium seeks young graduates from predominantly black schools and offers them the opportunity to earn a master's degree in business at any one of the five campuses. The program expects to generate about 100 graduates per year.

Stanford University's program is similar to the consortium. At Stanford, a summer preparatory program is envisioned. Funds are to be solicited from industry. The Stanford program takes two years to complete and plans to graduate about 10 students per year.

Harvard University's Graduate School of Business has created approximately 100 scholarships for black students. The Harvard program in early 1969 did not include a summer preparatory program.

Most programs are similar in that they seek young men and women with college degrees who express interest in business and enroll them in programs that lead to a master's. The only program that differs is one designed by the University of Massachusetts and dubbed ABLE (Accelerated Business Leadership Education). This program seeks young men or women currently employed in industry who have been identified by their firms as having the potential for advancement into upper echelons of management. Typically, the program takes fifteen months to complete. The initial summer session consists of an intensive program in the disciplines underlying business education. The employment of special instructional models will permit a high degree of flexibility in the design of curricula to meet individual needs.

Without question, the young black people currently employed in business or who are now pursuing business educations must prepare themselves to actively compete for the more responsible jobs in upper management. To do this adequately, the undergraduate education being offered at the predominantly black campuses must be upgraded. Some efforts are being made by industry to contribute to this uplift.

[1] The five schools are Indiana University, University of Rochester, University of Southern California, Washington University (St. Louis) and University of Wisconsin.

A concept known as the "cluster" has industry working very closely with black campuses and with black faculty. In a program designed by the Urban League, many faculty members from southern schools spend summers working in industry on meaningful projects. Industry also donated the time of staff members who visit campuses and serve as lecturers in their specialty.

All of these programs and projects serve the purpose of rapidly creating black executives to fill the contantly increasing demand. But even this surge will not be enough unless steps are taken to fill the pipelines with young people who must take on the management task tomorrow.

The Future Black Manager

It has been estimated that 100 jobs exist at the management level for every five trained black managers in existence. Any significant closing of this gap must await the crop of present high school students who must first be entitled to consider business as a career. The general disenchantment with business seems to be sweeping across college campuses where young graduates are looking at other options. This is due in part to the feeling that business does not offer them the challenge or the psychological reward that other pursuits might. With black students, the reasons might be the same, along with the feeling that business is not really serious about hiring and utilizing black people in meaningful jobs. The credibility gap is quite wide at present and from all indications nothing is being done to bridge it.

The gap is even wider in the high schools. The stimulus of black people in meaningful jobs in any large numbers serving as models to young people does not exist. The time to reach the future manager is when he is in high school, so that he can be headed down the road that will eventually lead into college and on into industry. The job can be left neither to counselors nor to luck. Industry must begin to do its own selling job. The first order of business must be a clear message to young black Americans that industry is receptive, that upward mobility is possible. This will require a combined effort on the part of industry, government, and educational institutions. The black managers who must take their place in business across the country must be competent. The creation of such managers in any meaningful numbers will require recruitment *now,* at the high school level.

It will take time. Until the pipeline is filled, business must attempt to survive with the interim programs suggested above. Failure to do the ground work now will only result in another crisis period in a few years.

Business has excluded non-whites, particularly blacks from industry participation for many years. The crisis situation we now face is a result of such exclusion. Planning is a management tool. Business is in a position to avoid the reoccurrence of this problem by making use of this fundamental rule of good business.

Dunbar S. McLaurin and
Cyril D. Tyson

10

The GHEDIPLAN for Economic Development

The past several summers have spawned events and tensions which have produced convincing proof that traditional approaches to the recurring urban crisis are woefully inadequate and that something new must be developed. It has become equally clear that any such new concept must be based upon creative economics. It must be something designed to increase the share of the economy held by ghetto residents.

The search has taken many different forms and has led the government, professional agencies, and the private sector into extensive searches for methods and means of devising this "something." A prime necessity is that it must be "instant." The ghettos must, in their own view, be made instantly more economically viable.

DUNBAR S. MCLAURIN *is the founder and president of a New York ghetto oriented consultant firm, Ghettonomics, Inc. A pioneer black economist, Dr. McLaurin has spent 25 years in the field of underdeveloped nations and ghetto economics. A member of the New York Bar, he has founded several businesses, including the only black-operated bank in New York State. He has served on advisory commissions to the United States Small Business Administration and several universities.*

CYRIL D. TYSON *is commissioner of Manpower and Career Development and deputy administrator of the Human Resources Administration, New York City. He has been executive director of the United Community Corporation in Newark, New Jersey, and executive director of HARYOU-ACT Inc. in New York City. A former director of the Business and Employment Division of the New York City Commission on Human Rights and project director for the Harlem Youth Opportunities Unlimited, Inc. document* Youth in the Ghetto, *Mr. Tyson has taught at Bronx Community College and Queens College.*

The most recent objective of this search, once it was narrowed down to the area of economics, has been described in such terms as "black entrepreneurship," "compensatory capitalism," "black capitalism," and the like. These approaches seem to have one thing in common—an effort to increase the economic capability and the financial resources of the black residents and other deprived populaces of the urban areas. This is seen as a partial solution to the recurring problems of the ghetto.

The weakness in this approach, however, is that it attacks basically only a portion of the problem. Development of ghetto or black entrepreneurship is desirable and laudable. But it must be tied into a network of infrastructures and super-structures which makes of entrepreneurship a productive function, rather than merely a *distributive* function. "Black capitalism," however defined, must be tied into the main economic system of the nation, or it will be meaningless. The development of management skills, the development of capital-accumulating institutions, the development of markets—all of these are items of great importance, but they achieve their importance only insofar as they become part of an entire economic system—i.e., insofar as they contribute to the *economic development* and *growth* of the ghetto.

If our objectives are limited merely to placing a few black men in business or to improving or slightly expanding the businesses of those black persons who already have businesses, then our objectives are too limited to achieve the goal of satisfying urban unrest. No less a goal can be defined for us than that of a realistic commitment to empowering the ghetto masses to grow into self-sufficiency through self-directed growth, creative change, and increased productivity. As so defined, it then becomes possible to see that our goal cannot be achieved unless we discard the piecemeal purely sociological cosmetic approaches of the past.

This new approach will lead us into the concept as expressed by Richard M. Nixon, long before he became President, namely, that the need is to "put the ghetto into business"—as contrasted with the earlier concept of "putting business into the ghetto," that is, moving large firms into the ghetto primarily to provide jobs.

Senator Jacob Javits, a pioneer in the field of ghetto economic development, has aptly stated the problem:

> The crux of this new trend of thought is that the remaking of the ghetto requires a total economic upgrading of the community itself, and that this, in turn, requires the ownership and control of new capital and business opportunity by people within the community.[1]

[1] "Big Business and The Ghetto," Jacob K. Javits. *New Generations,* vol. 50, No. 2, Spring 1968, National Committee on Employment of Youth, 145 E. 32 St. N.Y.C.

The problem has been that while there has been a general recognition of the necessity for remaking the ghetto, there has apparently not been a recognition of the total steps necessary to do so. Or where there has been that recognition, there has not been a willingness on the part of the white business and power structure to take those steps.

It is our view that nothing less than a complete restructuring of the ghetto economy will be sufficient to bring about the type of positive economic growth that can begin to raise the productivity of the blacks in such a manner that the burden on the urban economies will be lessened. Such a restructuring, in our view, can come about only by means of a total plan for ghetto economic development and industrialization. Such a plan would view the ghetto as a totality, as an underdeveloped nation, whose economic productivity and stability we wish to increase. The goal would be to redress the adverse balance of payments between the ghetto and the outer white world, and to attain capital and profits under local control and within the geographical area of the ghetto.

Inadequacies of Present Philosophy

The weakness in most ghetto economic development "plans," is that they are piecemeal approaches toward solving only a part of the problem. They fail to come to grips with such total problems of restructuring of the economy as the following:

Transferring ownership from absentee owners to local minority owners in an orderly manner, thereby retaining the economic input within the communities. Item: A recent report shows that 85 percent of the business volume in Harlem is done by white non-residents;

Developing an overall economic plan or framework through which the community can participate in the planning and systematic development of the community, while leaving the individual business development in the hands of individual enterpreneurs;

Diversifying, strengthening, and expanding the economic base of the ghetto so that it can compete in the wider economic mainstream; and

Increasing the "Ghetto National Product" (GNP) by increasing ghetto-owned industries that *produce,* as opposed to businesses that merely *distribute* "foreign" goods and services.

The absence of such considerations is the result of false assumptions related to the development of the ghetto. These assumptions are based upon a limited and proscribed view of the problem.

Some of the assumptions are:

First: that only research is needed to develop ghetto businesses. While this concept has recently been discarded, it very early resulted in a rash of "plans" which, when distilled, provided for nothing more than the collection of data about ghetto businesses. Many of these businesses failed even before the statistics were compiled. While research *is* needed, a study or a diagnostic survey is not the equivalent of economic development, nor does it alone produce such. It is, at most, a tool. Fortunately, this stage has almost been passed.

Second: that high unemployment is the real economic problem of the ghetto. This false assumption underlay the rash of "job development" plans. It is bottomed on the belief that if more people worked there would be more consumers, and ghetto businesses would therefore flourish. What is overlooked, however, is that these businesses are rarely *owned* by ghetto residents. This rash of "development plans," proved to be nothing more than programs to train, re-train, and break down employment barriers for the hard-core unemployed.

We hasten to point out that not every ghetto resident or minority person can become an entrepreneur. Moreover, such training and such jobs do produce desirable results, but these must not be taken as synonymous with overall economic growth.

Full employment is a desired goal and must be vigorously pursued, but it alone will not insure a healthy, viable, minority business community. The Negro had full employment on the plantation. Yet it insured only the economic growth of the white owner. New industry is needed in the ghetto. Manpower training is vital. Discrimination must end. But alone these are not the true routes to economic growth.

For without ownership and control of production and distribution, employment means little. The black man remains a straight man for the flow of money through him directly back into the white community. The minority business community must be helped to diversify and develop its capacity to own and control the economic mechanisms; to retain the money once it is earned, and to circulate the money within the community.

In the "real" world outside the ghetto, a dollar that is worth only a dollar is a losing dollar. A plan to develop the ghetto economically must look beyond mere full *employment*. The goal must be maximum *self*-employment. The ghetto must not only help provide full employment, it must also determine the multiplier-effect uses of money in the community and participate in the basic economic decisions that underlie a sound economy.

Third: that ghetto economic development requires only the provision of long-term, low-interest loan money. The theory is that only the lack of capital prevents the survival and expansion of the otherwise marginal and high-risk ghetto businesses.

Fourth: that the provision of management training, together with sufficient capital, is a sure-fire solution to the problem. All that is needed additionally, the theory goes, is some professional guidance about tax practices, and in the maintenance of ledgers, inventory systematizing, purchasing, store layout, etc.

These last two assumptions constitute perhaps the oldest and most traditional approach: provide the ghetto businessman with capital and training, and, ipso facto, the problem is solved. This approach is what we call the "old fur coat" theory, based upon the radio commercial: "If you remodel your old fur coat, you will still have an old fur coat."

It is apparent that if every minority businessman were thoroughly trained in bookkeeping, inventory control, layout, etc., and if each were given a small loan, the economy of the ghetto would hardly move upwards an inch. The result would be a community of clean, neat, tidy—but still marginal—shopkeepers with a minimum economic output. In short, we would still have "an old fur coat." The "old fur coat" approach has failed in minority economic development, largely because it itself is based upon a false assumption, namely . . .

Fifth: that minority businessmen have the same problems as their white counterparts and that remedies and legislation designed for the white community can be applied intact to the ghetto small business community.

The successful small businessman in the white community operates within a framework of mutually supporting larger businesses and industry. Unlike the minority businessman, he is an integral part of a fluid and mobile economy, in which he can move upwards and outwards in response to the interactions of the free enterprise system, and according to his own entrepreneurial ability. He is a member of a network of business and social relationships that are alien and unavailable to his minority counterpart but that constantly stimulate and offer him happenstance unearned opportunities. He has a heritage of business tradition and of easy availability of capital and technical know-how unknown to the ghetto. Growth is a natural consequence of this heritage; it is expected of the white businessman. And the rules and regulations of the game are designed for and by him.

The ghetto businessman has no such advantages, and no such opportunities. He operates within the high-walled framework of a closed economy. His access to the outer and larger business and industrial world with its opportunities, challenges, and stimuli is as non-existent as if he were in a remote, underdeveloped country.

Sixth: that the ghetto is a geographical area and that economic development must be confined to that area. This has resulted in the failure to recognize that because of the color label carried by most minority persons who are disadvantaged, such as blacks, Puerto Ricans, Mexican-Americans and others who have been discriminated against, the ghetto is wherever they are. The practical meaning of this is that we simply must address ourselves to increasing the productivity of all minority persons. The ghetto is more a *condition,* and a state of being discriminated against and left out of the mainstream, than it is a physically defined geographical area. While this renders the problem more complex, it also offers endless possibilities, such as introducing ghetto entrepreneurs to the ownership of viable businesses and industries regardless of the physical location.

As long as plans for the economic development of the ghettos are based upon such false assumptions as the foregoing, they will continue to fall far short of their goals, and of what is necessary to reach the problem. We are convinced that the problems of the ghetto economy must be viewed the same way as the problems of an underdeveloped nation are viewed—as an interlocking whole.

The GHEDIPLAN

This basic approach has led to the development by Mr. McLaurin of the Ghetto Economic Development and Industrialization Plan. This plan, called "GHEDIPLAN" for short, reflects the following basic philosophy:

The GHEDIPLAN views the ghetto as an underdeveloped nation, yielding an entirely different perspective than when the problems of the ghetto are viewed piecemeal. When the United States helps underdeveloped nations, it concentrates on extending the free enterprise system. The United States wants these nations to have a favorable balance of trade and applies hard and soft money theories in lending money at fair interest rates.

The goal is to create businesses and industries that will use local resources most productively. A central banking system, insurance networks, and other instruments of capital accumulation are established. Favorable tariff rates are set so these nations can trade with us, and production machinery as well as consumer items are sold. The goal, then, is to establish a balanced, diversified, and self-supporting economy that will generate capital and support a stable, friendly society. Enlightened and selfish dividends are sought, for only a stable economy can support a society that is free of political upheavals and friendly to us.

The parallel lesson for the United States is that ghettos are indeed impacted underdeveloped "nations." As long as their economies are unproductive, unstable, and unable to support their inhabitants in dignity, they, too, will breed upheavals. To eliminate our Wattses, Newarks, and Detroits, the cities' underdeveloped ghetto-nations must be given the economic tools with which to build stable and sound economies.

A final and fundamental similarity between the economic philosophy underlying both the GHEDIPLAN and aid programs for underdeveloped nations is that of "nationalism," the local ownership of the economy and the control of its destiny. This concept reflects the universal feeling that dignity, opportunity, and a sense of economic independence are vital energizing elements for the development of a young economy, whether in the ghetto or in an underdeveloped nation.

This, then, is the philosophic background for the GHEDIPLAN. It seeks to establish the machinery with which to restructure the ghetto economy in somewhat the same way we would restructure an underdeveloped nation. The plan would diversify the ghetto, create new businesses and industries, and interlock the whole with itself and with the presently "foreign" outer white community. It seeks to look at the overall ghetto picture and to utilize available municipal resources to create a whole new economy in the ghetto. This economy will be strong enough to participate in, compete with, and become an integral part of the national economy, contributing its own part to the Gross National Product, instead of being a "colonial" appendage. Against the backdrop of the times, nothing less seems worth trying. Nothing less will do.

INCREASING THE "GHETTO NATIONAL PRODUCT"

The ultimate objective of the GHEDIPLAN is to end poverty or sharply decrease it, by creating a strong, locally-owned economy that is integrated into the total economy. It will therefore increase the "GNP," by which we mean the Ghetto National Product. Emphasis is placed on those productive large-scale businesses and industries that will have a productive economic impact.

Although it could be applied and implemented by almost any large economic entity, such as a Chamber of Commerce, a State government, an Archdiocese, or any other similar unit, the plan was designed for a large urban city such as New York City or any one of its boroughs. We shall therefore use the city as the prototype to explain, briefly and generally, how the plan would operate.

In the place of a central governmental structure such as is found in an underdeveloped nation, the plan has devised instrumentalities which would allow the communities to participate in the economic planning, development, and growth of an area. The goal of the plan is to achieve economic growth without the need for large grants or any great cost to the city. The heart of the plan therefore is not grants but the pump-priming method of using the city's present fiscal, purchasing, and administrative resources in a new and creative manner. In short, it consists of re-directing the purchasing power and the fiscal deposit power of the cities, in such a manner as to generate economic activity in the ghetto.

The components are these:

Machinery

Administrative:	Office of Minority Economic Development
Operative:	Small Business Investment Companies (SBICs)
	Local Development Corporations (LDCs)
	Small Business Development Centers (SBDCs)
Supportive:	Private Economic Consultant Firm
	Small Business Administration

Tools

One:	"Guaranteed Markets" through a "set aside" policy of the City's purchases.
Two:	"Guaranteed Financing" through city "Link Deposits."

GUARANTEED MARKETS

A portion of the city's purchasing power will constitute a "Guaranteed Market" for new businesses and industries in the ghetto. For a city the size of New York for instance, with a half-billion dollar annual expenditure for purchases and small contracts, a set-aside of roughly 10 per cent of this amount could provide a substantial market for ghetto businesses. This would pump an estimated 50 million dollars of goods and services into the ghettos.

The example set by the public sector would in all likelihood trigger an equal flow from the private sector. A percentage of the vast purchasing power of foundations, trade associations, private industry, educational and religious institutions, social organizations, etc., could be redirected toward ghetto businesses and enterprises, almost as easily as the public sector had been. Other governmental purchases, such as federal and state, when added to the private sector, could easily provide another $50 million. There would thus exist a total Guaranteed Market of $100 million dollars.

As presently structured, however, minority small business communities cannot supply this demand, because they do not have the right type or the right size businesses. It is therefore necessary to diversify and restructure these ghetto economies by creating new businesses or expanding existing ones. Such a vast undertaking requires (1) ample capital and (2) technical and management training. These requirements are also supplied by the creative use of existing city resources, via Guaranteed Financing, and the machinery components described below.

GUARANTEED FINANCING

Guaranteed Financing in the City of New York could be achieved by using the city's aggregated $20 million to $100 million day-to-day demand deposits to encourage banks to lend money to, or invest in, minority businesses and industries.

The simple method of depositing the money without a particular "link" has been found to be unsatisfactory, as the mere promise of the bank to lend money is insufficient.

GHEDIPLAN would therefore extend and change the present unlinked policy. Each deposit would be *linked* to a specific commitment by the bank to lend or invest an agreed-upon amount. The line of credit thus established would be the ghetto's guaranteed financing, and the plan is designated the "Link-Deposit."

The city's non-interest bearing bank accounts, through the mechanism of "link-deposits" will induce banks to finance community "conduit corporations" which, with added federal SBA leverage funds will provide "Guaranteed Financing" for these businesses.

THE ADMINISTRATIVE MACHINERY

The Office of Minority Economic Development (OMED) would be the city's instrument to organize and catalyze the entire plan. It would represent the city in administering, implementing, and operating the plan, and would generate Guaranteed Financing and Guaranteed Markets with city resources.

THE OPERATIVE MACHINERY

Small Business Investment Companies (SBICs)—An SBIC is a conduit to convert city link-deposits into equity or venture capital. By securing matching federal funds, it will gain leverage of up to 3 to 1. SBICs are flexible enough to provide technical training and to be community-based, with one for each community, or they may be centralized with community branches and a common board.

Local Development Corporations (*LDCs*)—An LDC is a conduit to convert city link deposits into medium and long-term "brick-and-mortar" capital. These conduits will gain leverage of up to 9 to 1 by securing matching federal funds from SBA as set forth below. They are private, community-based and community-controlled. There would be one LDC in each community. Eventually, the LDC would be the economic planning center of the community, providing management and technical training and establishing businesses.

Small Business Development Centers (SBDCs)—are quasi-governmental, community-based economic development centers that will recruit, organize and spawn the LDC and SBIC ghetto conduits. Initially operational and administrative, they will provide training, technical aid and community coordination. While lack of government funds has caused SBDCs to be phased out in New York City, similar mechanisms can be developed to serve the same purpose with the help of foundations and other private resources. SBDCs now exist in many areas.

THE SUPPORTIVE MACHINERY

Private Economic Consultant Firm—Such a consultant firm would provide technical and professional know-how, presently lacking in the ghetto, for establishing the plan. It would provide back-up for management and technical training and would design and establish the two community "conduit corporations," the LDCs and the SBICs.

The Small Business Administration (SBA)—the federal SBA provides monetary leverage to both the LDC and the SBIC conduits through matching federal funding of up to 9 to 1. It provides a wide range of direct and guaranteed loans and of back-up technical services, advice, and materials.

OPERATIONAL CHRONOLOGY OF THE GHEDIPLAN

The City establishes an Office of Minority Economic Development. (OMED).

OMED retains a private economic consultant firm for technical back-up, especially in designing the conduits.

The firm works with the Small Business Development Centers (SBDCs), under OMED's supervision, to establish local conduit corporations and to plan the economic growth of the community.

OMED, aided by the consultant firm, establishes the procedure and machinery for the Guaranteed Markets and for the Link Deposits to provide Guaranteed Financing.

OMED, using Link Deposits, generates seed-money for the embryo conduits.

The conduits draw the seed money, hire staff and consult with an SBDC and the consulting firm to identify business opportunities and to organize the ownership structure of the proposed business.

The City's purchasing needs and link deposits are coordinated so that the new businesses are provided with Guaranteed Financing and Guaranteed Markets.

Under this chronology, the conduits are organized by OMED, experts from the consulting firm, and the SBDCs, each working together in an administrative, technical, and community operational capacity.

These conduits identify opportunities and organize new businesses or expand existing businesses, which are then backed up by management assistance and technical help from all levels. City purchases will provide their initial markets and city-generated funds their financing.

Since the conduits will be staffed by community persons, and their boards will come from the communities, their identification of projects will be locally oriented. They will, for instance, recognize the limitations, as well as the strengths of outside-sponsored franchising operations. Franchising is not the basic answer to local economic development; many franchises are just another type of outside "colonial" economic control. Such franchises limit local entrepreneurship and tie the economy to a basic pattern of retail distributorships, without any development of the supportive industries.

Communities also would be able to investigate the present trend toward the "sale and leaseback" type of deals, such as the Woolworth transaction in Harlem in 1968 described in chapter 8 by Mr. Hertz.

All in all, the conduit corporations would provide a valuable source of coordination of the various ingredients of the GHEDIPLAN. With this overall coordinated structure, chances for success of those ghetto businesses should be maximized.

COST AND FINANCING OF THE PLAN

The Plan's only foreseeable additional cost to the city would be that of creating the Office of Minority Economic Development and of retaining the services of the private economic consultant firm, since the Plan is designed to use the city's existing resources to generate up to $200 million in ghetto financing and new markets.

OMED would work directly with various Small Business Development Centers to establish the local conduits. Once a local conduit is operating, it will be self-supporting, and some will even generate a surplus.

The remaining cost is that of "start-up," or "seed-money," for the conduits. Seed money could come from a foundation or government grant. But the Plan prefers to avoid a grant, because it would diminish the objectives of self-help and self-sustaining private enterprise. Participating banks, therefore, would be asked for the seed money.

THE FUTURE OF THE GHEDIPLAN

The New York Urban Coalition has liberally borrowed the concepts of the GHEDIPLAN, and has set up a corporation to provide venture capital as was conceived in the Plan and has established a GHEDIPLAN-type management assistance corporation. Much of the administrative work is being done by the Coalition staff and task forces.

There are indications at present that at least two major cities will adopt the Plan in its entirety. This is welcomed by the authors, who hold a dim view of any piecemeal measures. The promise of the GHEDIPLAN lies in its establishment of an inter-relationship between the various economic segments in order to promote economic growth. A basic strength of the GHEDIPLAN is its facilitation of interaction and intermeshing in the economy, whereby Guaranteed Markets *support* businesses *created* by Guaranteed Financing and *guided* by SBDCs and other local conduit corporations.

It is interesting to note that because of the concepts set forth in the GHEDIPLAN the federal government has taken tentative steps toward a national guaranteed market and guaranteed financing as set forth in the Economic Opportunity Amendments of 1967. These amendments directed the OEO Director and Small Business Administrator to coordinate and cooperate with other federal agencies so that federal or federally-aided contracts, sub-contracts, and bank deposits are handled in a manner to bring economic regeneration to ghetto residents and small businessmen. Should this concept be implemented and adopted by the federal government, it is our belief that a new day will be seen in the economic life of the ghetto, and therefore in the life of the inner city.

*G. Douglas Pugh**

11

Bonding Minority Contractors

Background of the Problem

Black contractors have been the victims of exclusionary practices of the construction craft unions, which have, in the past, denied them entry into the construction trades. Today, because of their lack of experience and qualifications, too many black contractors are unprepared to participate in the benefits which will flow from the expected growth of the construction industry over the next decade from a 1960 level of $105 billion annually in new construction, maintenance, and repairs to $180 billion in the 1970s.[1]

These exclusionary practices have made it almost impossible for black workers to acquire construction skills and to enter the construction business through the normal channel of graduating from skilled worker and foreman into small scale contracting and then, with the accumulation of experience and capital, into larger and more complex work. It has also made it impossible for black contractors to have available to them the quantities of skilled workers needed for large enterprise. When to this pattern is added lack of access to financing, the result is an almost total inability of black contractors to qualify for surety bonds needed for participation in most FHA insured projects and on public construction work. A recent study[2] of seven major cities by the National Business League indicated that 67 per

---

* *This chapter was prepared in association with Matthew J. Domber, partner in Domber and Ward, a New York development consulting firm.*

[1] U.S. Industrial Outlook 1968 BDSA, Department of Commerce.

[2] National Business League—"Preliminary Analysis of Negro Contractors from Seven Cities," (Unpublished Memorandum) April, 1968.

cent of all minority contractors have been unable to obtain a single surety bond.

Thus, black contractors find themselves in a kind of circular trap where their lack of experience in bonded work makes it virtually impossible to obtain surety bonds for construction work requiring such bonds and thereby gain experience on this type of work, even though they might otherwise have the ability to perform.

Two actual cases illuminate the nature of the problem. In 1967, despite the offer of the Oakland Small Business Development Center to put up the money necessary to guarantee performance by a minority subcontractor unable to obtain a surety bond, the subcontractor who had submitted the lowest bid was rejected for the work by the general contractor on an Oakland public school construction project. When asked to intervene, the Oakland Board of Education refused to take action, citing a provision of California law[3] which gives a prime contractor the discretion to reject a bid from a subcontractor unable to furnish a bond from an admitted surety. The same problem faced a Negro construction company which had received a contract to build a $587,000 multipurpose health service center in Watts for the University of Southern California. The award was predicated upon the contractor's securing a surety bond. After a dozen rejections from surety companies, the University was finally persuaded to permit the contractor to proceed without a bond. It did so, but only after threats were made to burn down any building not constructed by a black contractor. The health center was successfully completed by the Negro contracting firm according to contract and is presently in operation.

But in all too many cases the minority firm never receives the opportunity to perform and often, even if given the opportunity, does not have the experience or financial capacity to engage in large-scale work. At this point in time, when a major thrust of our national housing program is to rebuild ghetto areas and the need for qualified black contractors to work in these areas is greater than ever, we find that there are very few black contractors who are eligible. There are approximately 870,000 general and specialty contractors in the United States.[4] In 30 states comprising 107 cities for which information on Negro contractors is available, it is estimated that no more than 1500–2000 black contractors are in business.[5] Most of these are small scale enterprises employing four workers or less, with an average construc-

[3] Government Code Section 4108.

[4] *Fortune* magazine, December, 1968—"The Unchecked Power of the Building Trades"—Thomas O'Hanlon.

[5] Ford Foundation list compiled from information received from individual minority contractors.

tion contract value of $20,000.[6] Simply to house new families and to replace the normal demolition of old housing units will require the construction of 20 million new dwellings over the next ten years. In addition, six million new or rehabilitated units are needed for lower income families now living in big city slums and slated for renewal under the Housing and Urban Development Act of 1968 and the Model Cities Program.

Ford Foundation Involvement

To help solve the problem that Negro and other minority contractors face, The Ford Foundation, in May, 1967, initiated discussions with surety companies in an effort to obtain their assistance in developing a program to qualify minority contractors for surety bonds. The Foundation addressed itself to this problem partly in response to requests for assistance from two sources: from minority contractors in various parts of the country and from representatives of the federal department of Housing and Urban Development who were concerned about the need to develop qualified black contractors to participate in urban redevelopment programs.

The Foundation viewed the problem as one of devising a program to bring minority contractors up to a standard that would permit them to engage competitively in the quest for business, and qualify in the ordinary course for surety bonds. The larger goal, as in other Foundation work toward expanding equal opportunity, is to "help talent to better help itself."

Contacts were made with the Surety Association of America, The American Insurance Association, and with three major surety companies: The Travelers Indemnity Company, The Hartford Insurance Group, and The Aetna Casualty and Surety Company. These companies expressed a willingness to cooperate in the design of a program to develop increased Negro contractors' bonding capacity. They made it clear, however, that while desiring to render every assistance, they would not bond a contractor unless they felt reasonably certain that the contractor had the experience, organizational and financial capacity to undertake and satisfactorily complete the project. In their view, the construction business was risky even under the best of circumstances—with a relatively high rate of failure—without encouraging inexperienced or undercapitalized contractors to engage in it.

They also believed that the problem facing minority contractors, in addition to the one of insufficient financial resources, was inexperience

[6] National Business League—"Preliminary Analysis of Negro Contractors from Seven Cities," April, 1968.

and lack of managerial capacity, which could not be solved merely by making capital available.

This point of view, as expressed by professional surety men, was succinctly stated in a position paper entitled, "The Surety Industry and Minority Group Contractors," prepared by the American Insurance Association in October, 1968. (Unpublished memorandum.)

> Absolute candor compels us to point out that the chief and recurring difficulty which most minority group contractors encounter in applying for surety bonds arises from their marked deficiencies in experience, management and other skills in running construction jobs of more than limited scope. While very many also lack working capital to a certain degree, with the availability of financing through such governmental sources as the Small Business Administration coupled with various lending techniques, such financial weakness is often secondary to lack of expertise. . .
>
> . . . We believe that it will serve no useful purpose, economic or sociological, for surety companies to issue contract bonds indiscriminately to all applicants, qualified or not. Such an unqualitative underwriting policy will unquestionably undermine the present confidence of owners in contract surety bonds. It will not only anger owners left with unfinished projects, but will also inflict a mortal wound on the performance reputation of minority group contractors as a class.

In addition to providing an understanding of the industry viewpoints, these contacts with the surety industry have led to the establishment of an informal channel for looking into complaints by minority contractors who have been rejected for surety bonds. In one case, inquiry to a surety company which had allegedly rejected the application of a New Orleans contracting firm for a bond for a $2,700,000 FHA project, revealed that the application had never been forwarded by the local surety agent to the company. When made aware of this, the company suggested the name of another local agent to process the application. The contractor had substantial experience, a net worth in excess of $500,000 and an irrevocable letter of credit from a local bank for $200,000. The bond was written.

The Oakland Model

The three-year Oakland demonstration program was sponsored by the General and Specialty Contractors Association of Oakland, California, an organization of some sixty minority general and specialty contractors, in cooperation with the Oakland Small Business Development Center, the Management Council for Bay Area Employment Opportunity and the Alameda County Building and Construction Trades Council.

The development of the program was assisted by a feasibility study conducted by Kaiser Engineering and was further refined as the result of processing a test case with the cooperating San Francisco surety company representatives. It called for the formation of a Contractor's Assistance Board to supervise the operation of a supportive assistance program for minority contractors and to engage an appropriate professional staff and consultants necessary to service the assistance program.

The pilot project had four elements:

(1) The organization of general and specialty contractors in the community into a trade association through which they could be reached and aided. The association serves at the same time as a conduit for the dissemination of information to the contractors about the programs being developed to assist them, and as an organizational vehicle for membership participation in these programs. It plays a major role in:

—seeking out construction opportunities for its members;
—referring these opportunities to eligible members;
—cataloging the skills and capabilities of its members;
—sharing common problems and providing, through mutual assistance, for their solution;
—securing federal and other funds for educational and training programs;
—bringing together consortia to perform contracts beyond the unaided skills and abilities of a single member;
—undertaking the development of projects such as "turnkey" public housing projects which could provide job opportunities for its members;
—contacting and negotiating with various government agencies about construction contract opportunities;
—representing the various interests of the contractors in the contractor assistance program and with other construction industry trade associations.

The constructive roles which could be played are limitless.

(2) The provision of technical assistance at the level of general instruction and at the level of supervising the performance of a particular job and, if necessary, being prepared to actually take over its operation. This has been accomplished through the establishment of a Contractors' Assistance Board composed of minority contractor representatives and members drawn from the business and financial community experienced in the problems of the construction industry. Serving on the Oakland board, in addition to representatives of the minority contractors trade association, are:

—a business executive presently serving as the director of a non-profit organization to promote economic opportunities for minorities in the San Francisco Bay area;

—a senior construction loan officer of the Bank of America;
—a senior construction vice-president of Kaiser Engineering;
—the director of Oakland Small Business Development Center, Inc.;
—the Business Representative of the Alameda County Building and Construction Trades Council;
—the Assistant Secretary of the Carpenters Bay Counties District Council;
—the Executive Director of the Human Rights Commission in San Francisco.

(3) The provision of adequate financing so that the contractor has available a ready credit source to permit the job to be properly financed and to enable him to have the liquidity and "quick assets" which a surety company would require for bonding. In a non-bonded job the same cash requirements would exist to insure that a proper flow of money on the job would be available. This financing was supplied in Oakland by a grant of funds to be loaned to the contractors on a basis subordinate to the sureties.

(4) Through its paid expert staff of accountants, cost estimators, construction specialists, its ability to engage first rank consultants and the skills of its board members, the Contractors Assistance Board can provide assistance to a contractor on a particular job in:

—accounting and record keeping;
—cost estimating;
—locating proper subcontractors and skilled labor;
—preparing and submitting bids;
—preparing proper construction contracts and documents;
—organizing the job site and supervising the job;
—determining the cash flow requirements of the job;
—administering job funds through a blocked account;
—establishing proper relationships with trade unions and government agencies concerned with the job;
—finding and hiring proper skilled foremen, supervisors, and craftsmen;
—insuring that job proceeds are properly received and applied to the job, etc.

In short, the project seeks to help in the performance of every conceivable function that could be required for a successful job. In its role as the supplier of assistance, the board also serves to screen out obviously unsuited contractors and attempts to guide contractors toward jobs within their aided capacity and which will permit reasonable and orderly growth.

The Board also is constituted in a manner that will generate confidence on the part of surety companies that might bond any of the contractors. This will be done by assuring that proper business management and experience will be available to assist the contractor in carrying out the job, which is important if the contractors are to be helped in performing bonded work.

The Oakland project received a $300,000 grant from the Ford Foundation in June, 1968, of which $150,000 was to provide a revolving fund for the purpose of making financing available to satisfy the "quick assets" needed for bonding eligibility. The remaining $150,000 was to be used to pay the salaries of the program manager and staff for a three-year period. An additional $105,000 was subsequently granted in December 1968 to cover additional operating expenses and the employment of consulting services. In addition, a grant of $75,000 was made by the Economic Development Administration of the Department of Commerce for the strengthening and support of The General and Specialty Contractors Association, the minority contractors trade association.

The Oakland Performance

Between its inception in June, and December, 1968, the Oakland program loaned or committed to contractors $110,000, which has aided them in securing construction work valued at almost $1.5 million—most of which has involved bonded work and none of which would have been possible without the assistance provided by the bonding program. This six-months record compares well with initial hope that the program would generate about $4 million a year in additional construction volume—doubling the 1967–68 volume of GSCA members.

Some of the different accomplishments of the project include:

—obtaining a bond on a $250,000 contract for a general contractor whose largest previous bond had been $80,000;

—obtaining a bond on an $80,000 job for an electrical subcontractor who had never been bonded before;

—assisting a minority contractor to develop a "turnkey" project for the Oakland Housing Authority;

—assisting eight contractors who had never bid on public work before to obtain bonds and to submit bids (These contractors having been shown how to proceed are now beginning to bid on their own without assistance. One contractor was a successful bidder and others have placed second and third in the bidding process);

—arrangements have been made to have contractors qualified to bid on local university construction and to receive notice of prospective work; and

—lines of communication have been opened with local surety company representatives which have resulted in bonding acceptance on every application submitted by a contractor who has used the facilities of the project to develop a set of books and records and a current financial statement.

On the basis of the encouraging signs in the Oakland Project and the positive response from the Surety Industry regarding the approach to the problem, The Ford Foundation has initiated similar projects in three other cities: Cleveland, Boston, and New York.

Other Cities

CLEVELAND

In Cleveland the project was organized under the sponsorship of The PATH Association, a private non-profit civic organization established to foster the development of programs to improve the quality of housing, planning, and community development in the Greater Cleveland area and to provide a clearinghouse for information and citizen participation. The project has the support of the Insurance Board of Cleveland (and its Suretyship Subcommittee), the Cleveland Homebuilders Association, The Greater Cleveland Growth Association, The Businessmen's Interracial Committee on Community Affairs, and the Greater Cleveland Associated Foundation. It is also supported by the Society of Registered Contractors, an association of more than 78 Negro contractors and subcontractors, the organization of which was stimulated by the proposed establishment of the Bonding Program. The total funding for the three-year program is $645,000. A Ford Foundation grant of $225,000 made in January, 1969, was to be utilized at the rate of $20,000 in the first year and $102,500 per year for the next two years. The Economic Development Administration of the Department of Commerce has granted $100,000 to The PATH Association, of which $80,500 will be used for salaries and operating expenses for the Bonding Program and $19,500 for a three-month construction and maintenance training program during the first year with anticipated additional grants of $35,000 per year in the second and third years of the program. A revolving loan fund for contractors of $150,000 will be locally funded from the Cleveland NOW! program, a ten-year program of $1.5 billion primarily concerned with job development and better housing in Cleveland. Funds have been raised and committed from individuals, industry, and civic groups and federal funds. Cleveland NOW! is administered by Mayor Carl B. Stokes. It is anticipated that an additional $100,000 for the revolving fund will be provided by the Hough Development Corporation.

NEW YORK

In New York City, AUCOA (the Association of United Contractors of America) is a non-profit organization comprised primarily of 60 black and Puerto Rican contractors, but also including members of the allied professions, such as architects, engineers, and suppliers. It has established a subsidiary Contractors Accreditation and Control Board (CACB) which will have the responsibility for administering and conducting the Bonding Project. In setting up this Board, AUCOA reserved the right to participate in the selection of non-AUCOA members in order to maintain AUCOA's integrity and to form a Board sympathetic to the aims of the project. Serving on the Board, in addition to AUCOA representatives are: a construction loan officer of the Chase Manhattan Bank; the manager of the Bonding Department of Travelers Insurance Company; a professor from Columbia University School of Architecture; an attorney from the New York City Human Resources Administration; a construction lawyer and two insurance executives. The New York City project is funded for three years for a total of $935,000. The Economic Development Administration of the Department of Commerce has granted $135,000 to CACB for technical assistance for the first year with anticipated additional grants of $135,000 per year in the second and third years of the program. The Model Cities Program has granted $120,000 for a start-up fund to CACB for the first year. A Ford Foundation grant of $210,000 will go to AUCOA at $70,000 per year for three years, and an additional $50,000 grant for the Revolving Loan Fund. The New York City Urban Coalition will provide the remaining $150,000 for the Revolving Loan Fund.

BOSTON

The Boston project was organized through the efforts of the Eastern Gas and Fuel Associates in conjunction with the Contractors Association of Boston (CAB), a non-profit organization representing approximately thirty-five black and Spanish-speaking contractors. The format is the same as in other cities and the program is funded for three years for a total of $892,550. EDA will contribute $130,850 for the bonding program during the first year with anticipated similar grants in the second and third years. The Model Cities Program will contribute $150,000 for the Revolving Fund and the Urban Foundation of Boston will grant an additional $50,000 to the Revolving Fund. The Ford Foundation will grant $300,000 for three years to support the CAB trade association.

The project has been endorsed by the Surety Underwriters Association of Massachusetts, the local Small Business Administration and the financial and business community. There is a good possibility that a consortium of banks will create a revolving loan fund for contractors to secure loans utilizing Small Business Administration guarantees provided a subordination agreement acceptable to the surety companies can be worked out.

By January 1969, The Ford Foundation had issued 5,000 copies of a *Manual of Organizational Steps and Procedures for the Establishment of a Minority Contractor Bonding Program* which was based upon the Oakland experience. The hope was that it would serve both as a stimulus and a tool for individuals and organizations interested in sponsoring similar programs throughout the country.

The overall response to the announcement of the program and the requests for similar assistance from minority contractors in almost every major urban area make clear the acceptability of the program to the minority community and the need for a program of this type on a national basis. It also indicates the need for a National Minority Contractors Institute which would perform, at the national level, all of the functions of a national trade association and would help to organize and develop local contractors' assistance programs where need might exist. Such an institute could join minority contractors' representatives with representatives of the business and construction communities who could make available professional assistance and access to the resources of their respective industries. Preliminary discussions along these lines have been held by representatives of:

The National Technical Association;
The National Association of Home Builders;
The Associated General Contractors of America;
The Mortgage Bankers of America;
The American Sub-Contractors Association;
The National Retail Lumber and Building Material Dealers;
The National League of Insured Savings Association; and
The U.S. Savings and Loan League.

New Opportunities

Although the initiative in this endeavor should be taken by the private sector, the vast resources of federal programs in the construction field hold a broad range of productive opportunities for action now—action that could make a measurable impact on the development of black entrepreneurship. In October 1968 a federal government Committee on Federal Construction Contracts and Programs began working intensively on developing ways to make federal programs a more effective tool in upgrading minority contractors. For example:

(1) Supplemental funds of the *Model Cities Program* could be used in:

—training prime or subcontractors in management skills;
—providing a revolving fund for working capital to meet overhead costs;
—providing a revolving fund for equity capital; and

—assisting non-profit organizations to act as sponsors of projects providing construction opportunities.

(2) Section 3 of the 1968 *Housing and Urban Development Act* calls for maximum feasible utilization by professional businesses of architects, planners, builders, contractors, etc., owned or partly-owned by persons residing in the project area. These businesses are to be used to perform planning, construction or rehabilitation as prescribed by HUD under Sections 235, 236; Section 221 (d) (3) of the National Housing Act; and the low rent housing program under the Housing Act of 1937.

(3) *FHA Insurance and Subsidy Programs.* The effect of Section 3 on the FHA program may require sponsors to certify that the contractor has made efforts to use subcontractors located in the neighborhood or that FHA give preference to sponsors using minority contractors under Section 221 (d) (3), 221 (h) and the new 235 and 236 programs.

(4) *HAA (Housing Assistance Administration) Turnkey Public Housing.* Associations of minority contractors or minority development corporations can prepare proposals and participate in the Turnkey Program. Under the turnkey procedures for the low rent public housing program, private developers submit site and development plans for a housing project to the local housing authority. With HUD approval, the developer builds and equips buildings and then turns the key over to the local housing authority when the project is completed. The opportunities should be excellent since local housing authorities, because of the provision of Section 3, will have to show their efforts to solicit and employ neighborhood-based contractors in all public housing construction.

(5) *RAA (Renewal Assistance Administration).* Under the Renewal and Neighborhood Development Program, a developer can be selected who will maximize the objectives of minority contractor participation.

(6) *New Communities.* Under Section 409 of the New Communities Act (Title IV of the Housing and Urban Development Act of 1968), the Secretary may adopt requirements which encourage the use of small builders in the New Communities Program. Non-discrimination provisions would assure that minority builders have adequate representation in the program.

(7) *MDTA (Manpower Development & Training Act, The Department of Labor).* Programs can include managerial training and technical assistance to minority contractors, plus liberalizing the *MA 4 Program* (under which the government compensates employers for the costs of training entry-level employees) to facilitate the use of MA 4 funds by minority contractors who have limited capital. Special Impact Funds could be utilized for grant equity to provide venture money to entrants into the contracting field.

(8) *OEO (Office of Economic Opportunity).* Under Title I of the Economic Opportunity Act, these programs can generally be used for any community purpose to provide training and other assistance where the importance of community action can be justified. Similarly, the New Careers Program under Section 205 (e) of the OEO Act might be used for upgrading the skills of minority contractors or in developing the skills of promising candidates, although this program has not generally been used for this purpose, but rather has been focused on upgrading employee skills to sub-professional levels.

(9) *Small Business Administration.* In addition to its power to guarantee business loans to contractors (particularly loans subordinated to sureties to permit contractors obtaining such loans to qualify for surety bonds), the SBA under Section (8) (a) of the SBA Act can subcontract with minority contractors for federal construction work. Section (8) of the SBA Act authorizes SBA to enter into contracts with federal agencies obligating it to furnish supply articles to the government and to perform such contracts by subcontracting with small business concerns or others. It may be possible for the SBA contracting officer to enter into construction contracts with military and civilian agencies for appropriate projects mutually selected with such agencies. These contracts would fall into two classes—*limited* and *large* projects. In the *limited* projects SBA would contract directly with qualified minority contractors. In the *large* projects, SBA could contract with large contractors and require them to subcontract to "disadvantaged" contractors to the maximum extent feasible. As the prime contractor, SBA could assure compliance with this requirement.

(10) *EDA (Economic Development Administration, Department of Commerce).* EDA makes funds available in three categories with the overall purpose of eliminating unemployment.

The three categories of assistance are:

Public Works	\$606 million
Business Loans	\$138 million
Technical Assistance and Planning	\$ 9 million

(Dollar amounts indicate funds allotted over a three year period.) Committee on Federal Construction Contracts Memorandum HUD-95 (7-65), Nov. 14, 1968, p. 7. The committee final report noted that bonding requirements are less stringent for all contracts of less than \$2,000. The writer feels that this figure should be substantially higher, with the federal government thereby assuming the role of self-insurer for a larger number of minority contractors.

EDA guarantees 90 per cent of the working capital on projects they approve.

The federal programs enumerated and the approaches indicated are just a beginning.

The organization and implementation of a contractor's bonding program on a national scale gives promise of making available to minority contractors meaningful participation in the construction opportunities ahead. Such a program can create access to the construction industry not only for minority general and subcontractors, but also for thousands of minority adults and youths who are now excluded from the building trades unions. In addition, increased construction opportunities for black people can spawn growth and opportunity in many related fields: better housing and community development programs; opportunities in real estate development and ownership; in banking, mortgage, and surety brokerage, and insurance; and in real estate management and brokerage, law, accounting, and other fields.

This wide spectrum of opportunity adds up to a challenge—the challenge of harnessing the available resources, not merely to rebuild the cities, but to develop in the process new sources of economic strength within the black communities.

Martin Skala

12

Inner-City Enterprises: Current Experience

The Ghetto Plant Approach

At a time when most industry is marching to the outskirts of metropolitan America, a growing number of companies are plunging into the midst of the ghetto ferment. They are testing out a new kind of government-business partnership aimed at relieving urban poverty with jobs and capital. So far the movement back to the inner city is hardly more than a noble experiment. Few of the results are yet measurable, except that some jobs have been created and lots of red ink spilled.

Controversy surrounds industry's efforts to pour new resources into the ghetto. Some black militants charge ghetto plants are "instant concrete plantations," reflecting a new style of economic colonialism. Skeptics in the corporate ranks doubt inner-city manufacturing units can be viable over the long run without indefinite injections of government aid. And federal officials, uncertain of how much aid the government can afford to give, are debating whether it should be in the form of tax incentives, manpower training grants, or some other combination.

Most of the two dozen ghetto plants established in the past 2 years are modest in size, involving investments of \$1 million to \$2 million and

---

MARTIN SKALA *is a business and financial correspondent for the* Christian Science Monitor. *He has been a financial analyst with American Cyanamid Company, and served as Afro-Asian editor for* Business International. *He is the author of many articles on black economic development.*

geared to turn out relatively unsophisticated products. The number of jobs provided has been relatively small, probably not more than 8,000. On the other hand, most firms are still phasing trainees into their operations and have not reached their peak employment. In 1969 many companies were still sitting on the fence, waiting to assess the experience of the pioneers before making up their minds.

THE OUTLOOK IN LATE 1968

Some examples show the variety of ghetto projects announced in 1968.

Avco was building a $2.8 million printing facility in Boston's Roxbury area to supply the diversified aerospace company with a wide range of printed materials formerly purchased from external sources. The plant was designed to employ about 200 people, mostly drawn from the ranks of the hard-core unemployed. Instead of giving the construction contract to a big white contractor, Avco set up a consortium of 9 black contractors, most of whom had never undertaken a major building project.

Control Data was putting up small plants in Minneapolis and in Washington, D.C. The two facilities were intended to produce specialized components for the rapidly expanding computer maker's own manufacturing organization. Employment was expected to reach about 600 people.

Westinghouse was installing a $1 million plant in Pittsburgh's Homewood-Brushton section to make small industrial trucks. It was leasing the plant from a local black-owned, non-profit economic development corporation.

EG&G Roxbury Inc., a diversified instrumentation firm, had opened a metal fabricating plant in Boston's Roxbury slum. EG&G intended to employ 200 Roxbury blacks when in full gear. An unusual feature of the venture was a long term divestiture arrangement.

Xerox was assisting FIGHT (Freedom, Integration, God, Honor, Today), a militant black organization in Rochester, N.Y. to establish a wholly-owned enterprise that is projected to grow into a $1 million a year business. Employing about 100 people, the enterprise called FIGHTON (see below) was to make electrical transformers and metal stampings. For the first two years Xerox had contracted for $1.2 million of all the output. A $450,000 Labor Department manpower grant lowered start-up costs to a nominal figure, permitting the venture to be 100 per cent debt-financed.

THE CORPORATION AND THE COMMUNITY

A look at corporate approaches in setting up a ghetto enterprise reveals a mixed pattern. Some companies have acquired land, factory space, and a work force with little or no prior consultation with ghetto leaders. Where a company has moved into the ghetto suddenly, without explaining its goals and motives clearly to the community, there has often been a ground swell of resentment bordering on hostility. Some managements however are sensitive to rising aspirations for economic self-determination. Xerox, for example, brought the FIGHT organization into its early planning sessions. Policies affecting management control, product mix, hiring, and ultimate ownership were hammered out in lengthy joint meetings.

The question of community control is often a thorny issue. Most companies assume they will be welcomed for the new job opportunities they provide. They overlook the community's desire for a voice in management and a share in the ownership. Increasingly, companies are faced with a stubborn demand for a "piece of the action," as the price of winning support among ghetto leaders. Thus several companies such as Aerojet-General, EG&G, and Warner-Swasey are planning to share ownership of the enterprise with employees and the community. A few others including Xerox and GE avoided the potentially explosive issue by not taking an equity stake in the project at all. Instead, they gave free managerial, marketing, and technical assistance to a community group which in turn raised the "seed money" and a management team.

A key to financing this type of venture is usually a guaranteed market for the first few years of output. As black community groups rarely have any capital at their disposal, a powerful corporate sponsor is an indispensable aid in raising outside financing. The financing agency looks to the sponsor as a moral, if not legal, guarantor to secure the loan. One of the best forms of collateral is a long-term purchasing contract with the sponsor. This assures the fledgling business of a steady source of revenue during the difficult "break-in" stage.

Most companies are willing to settle for a smaller than normal return on their ghetto operations. Even with government manpower training grants to subsidize training of the "hard-core," corporate officials say the profit outlook is far from rosy.

Ghetto plants face high costs across the board, from labor to land. Inner-city land is more expensive than a plot in suburbia, taxes are steeper, and insurance rates costlier. Westinghouse, for example, says it will pay about $70 in tax for each $1,000 of investment in its Pittsburgh industrial truck facility, about triple the figure the company normally pays in non-urban areas.

A BLACK WORK FORCE

Despite a boost from manpower training grants, upgrading the "hard-core" is a formidable challenge. Labor costs are substantially higher than the wage rate alone might indicate, and many companies start trainees at more than the $1.60 minimum wage.

But the wage does not reflect the big overhead charges—indirect costs stemming from absenteeism, high turnover, and an enormous supervisory effort. A profile of the workforce at Aerojet-General's Watts Manufacturing Co., a plant set up in the aftermath of the Watts riots, gives some idea of industry's challenge: ten to fifteen per cent were virtually illiterate; ninety per cent had never held a steady job; and the average man had at least three arrests and a felony conviction. During its first year, Watts hired 1,000 people to retain a staff of 500, a turnover of 100 per cent. Turnover still runs as high as 45 per cent a year.

Not all ghetto plants have picked up as disadvantaged a group as Watts Manufacturing. Nevertheless, absenteeism, a high turnover rate, and lack of discipline are common complaints among ghetto plant managers. Almost all training programs have had to expand beyond basic job skills into remedial education, financial counselling, and other kinds of specialized advisory services. Before a man is ready to hold up his end of the production line, a four- or five-month training period is often required.

To defray the "extraordinary" expenses incurred in taking on the hard-core, business has relied principally on manpower training grants from Washington. These grants provided by the Labor Department range from about $1,000 to more than $5,000 per man, depending on the length and complexity of the training cycle. In some cases, such as Control Data's Minneapolis plant, a manpower grant has been equivalent to anywhere from 15 to 20 per cent of the company's total investment in the new facility.

The "cultural shock" which comes from imposing the discipline of an industrial environment on the hard-core unemployed often takes a long time to overcome. Meeting production deadlines and delivery schedules is difficult, at least until the plant workforce stabilizes.

The psychological insecurity of the hard-core, notes Robert Earle, general manager of Avco-Roxbury, makes it almost impossible for them to think in terms of long-term career goals. Instead, they view employment as a day-to-day job. Because they have done only menial work in the past, learning the importance of "the need to produce" is a painstaking process.

Most ghetto plant managers believe it is a mistake to hire a high percentage of the hard-core without surrounding them with a cadre of experienced workers. The hard-core must have some "good examples to relate to," maintains Melvin Barmat, Fairchild Hiller executive. One of Fairmicco's first mistakes, according to Mr. Barmat, was hiring hard-core exclusively, instead of trying to get a mixture of skilled and unskilled workers. Fairmicco is a joint venture between Fairchild Hiller, a leading aero-space firm and the Model Inner City Community Organization of Washington, D.C.'s Shaw area. The 60 man plant was the first to be started in the capital after the spring 1968 riots.

BLACK MANAGEMENT

The avowed goal for most ghetto plants, in theory at least, is community management. In practice this goal may be hard to realize, even allowing for the shakedown period when the company is run by people from the sponsoring firm.

Even for the largest firms, recruiting capable black managers and first-line supervisors is not easy. To some extent, aerospace companies have a head start. Equal opportunity clauses in defense contracts have opened the doors to Negroes wider here than in most industries. Yet many aerospace companies have groups of Negro engineers and technicians but few Negro administrative or managerial personnel.

Avco-Roxbury's eight executive slots were initially filled by whites, but within a year they had trained black replacements. EG&G-Roxbury was able to hire Negroes to fill several management spots. Rochester's FIGHTON boasts an all-black management team headed by an ex-barbershop proprietor who was recruited from within the ranks of FIGHT. Besides purchasing most of the firm's output for 2 years, Xerox has agreed to provide a full-time manufacturing expert, a financial analyst and other technical advice.

Fairchild-Hiller spent many months looking for a Negro with managerial credentials to steer Fairmicco. After a prolonged search, and an easing of the job's qualifications, Fairchild picked a retired Air Force Lieutenant Colonel. The company discovered that the armed forces was one of the few career fields in which a capable Negro could readily move up into positions of responsibility. The retired officer did not work out, however, and several more months were lost in finding another black manager. To close the managerial gap, Fairmicco in 1968 sent six men through a Department of Commerce-funded management trainee program.

PRODUCTS AND MARKETS

In setting up ghetto plants, one of the primary concerns is determining the right product—one with a ready-made market, not too complicated to make, and involving skills with a fairly wide range of applicability.

To avoid the inevitable delays associated with seeking new markets, many firms are using ghetto plants as a source of supply for internal needs. International Business Machines' Bedford-Stuyvesant operation, for example, makes computer cables, a fairly labor-intensive product needed throughout IBM's manufacturing organization.

Avco-Roxbury is turning out a variety of printed materials for the parent company's 15 divisions. The ambitious Avco goal is to qualify the hard-core as full journeymen in the printing trades. If the unions recognize this training as the equivalent of a traditional apprenticeship program, the workers will be able to take their skills anywhere in the country and earn up to $12,000 annually.

Watts Manufacturing originally hoped to make electronic components for Aerojet-General. But it was soon apparent that too high a level of sophistication was required. The company started off with a $2.5 million government contract to make 5,000 army tents. It has since branched out into wooden shipping containers, metal fabrication and some electronic work. Government orders currently account for only about 60 per cent of Watts' $4 million annual volume. Future growth is expected to come primarily from the private sector.

Government contracts are often the most appealing source of new business for the ghetto plants. They involve few selling costs and product specifications are ordinarily well-defined. Potential borrowers with a government contract in hand find it is much easier to get long-term financing from banks and other institutions. Moreover, a provision of the Small Business Act permits SBA to favor small untried suppliers in bidding on government contracts. Within limits, the SBA can distribute small business set-aside contracts originating with other agencies.

Yet government contracts, notes Melvin Barmat, of Fairchild Hiller, can be a "mixed blessing." They typically do not allow for much profit. And federal procurement officials, armed with detailed performance standards, can be very demanding taskmasters for an inexperienced management and work force. When Fairmicco was originally set up, Model Inner City Community Organization, the majority partner, did not want the company to be captive supplier to the aerospace firm. After a lengthy debate, Fairchild Hiller agreed to launch the company with wooden pallets as the major product. Fairmicco signed an SBA contract for 50,000 wooden shipping pallets. The decision was based on two facts. The government uses many pallets in the Washington area and pallet manufacturing is a growing industry. Fairmicco hopes the trainees' wood-working know-how will lead to future orders in the furniture field, thereby providing some upward mobility for the workers.

The preferential treatment implied by SBA set-asides does not always materialize. At the beginning of 1969, EG&G-Roxbury was counting on an SBA set-aside contract as a significant portion of its first year's business. When a competitor won the contract with a bid that was far lower, the company had to hastily restructure its manufacturing organization. None of the 50 hard-core trainees were dropped, but EG&G was forced to merge the ghetto company with a bigger subsidiary in order to sustain production and cut down overhead expenses.

Realizing the unpredictable nature of government work, many companies are searching for commercial business. EG&G-Roxbury, which opened with a GE subcontract to make aircraft engine stampings, looks to commercial metal fabricating for expansion. It reckons that developing a proprietary product line may take as long as three to five years.

Watts Manufacturing has doggedly reduced its share of government business to about 60 per cent over a 3-year span. At the same time, tent-making is beginning to fall off. The diversification effort has not been too successful, however, and the firm has yet to earn a profit on a sustaining basis.

DIVESTITURE

A number of ghetto plants are founded on the premise that they will eventually be independent units, owned and managed largely by minority group members. Over a period of time, the sponsoring companies expect to withdraw their personnel and resources, hopefully at a modest profit. At least one company has spelled out a long-term divestiture program, the first step being a generous employee stock option plan. It envisons a public stock offering with the black community once the venture has achieved a solid record of profitable operations.

Probably the most widely watched of the new ghetto operations, Watts Manufacturing, plans to offer an employee stock option plan allowing them to buy up to 51 per cent of the company. While demand for stock options has come primarily from managerial ranks, Watts hopes the idea of equity ownership will eventually catch on among the rank and file.

But until ghetto plants overcome their growing pains, managers see dangers in encouraging community ownership. They are fearful that ghetto residents may wind up with a poor investment, one which will yield slim returns, or might go sour. While early divestiture is urged by black militants, corporate officials consider such demands unrealistic.

In Fairmicco's case, hopes of an early public offering were dashed when business losses began escalating at a faster pace than anticipated. Originally, the backers wanted to issue 100,000 shares at $1 apiece in the Shaw area. The purpose was to enlarge the company's skimpy $15,000 equity base, at the same time reducing Fairchild's ownership slice substantially. A registration statement that had been filed with the SEC was withdrawn when it became apparent that serious managerial and production problems were not going to be resolved quickly. "How can you ask the ghetto to buy stock when losses are piling up?" said Mr. Barmat.

To set the business on its feet, Fairchild has had to sink additional capital into the project as well as scrap its timetable for withdrawal. Originally, the aerospace company had planned to retire most of its managerial and technical support within a year or two.

A less hurried but probably more realistic divestiture plan is being tried by EG&G. It talks of reducing its equity gradually over a 20-year period. In the first phase, the emphasis is on building up employee ownership. Sometime after the fifth year a public offering is envisioned. The offering would wait until the business was firmly established under a seasoned black management and the stock had some tangible value. Fifty-five per cent of the stock is earmarked for management and employees, while 20 per cent will be allocated to the public. EG&G's share will shrink to 25 per cent at the end of 20 years. It plans to retain control throughout the formative trial and error period. After a year's service, employees become eligible to purchase stock at $1 a share over a four year span. The amount of shares allocated each employee is determined by his pay scale.

Sometime after the fifth year, voting control would pass from EG&G to the managers and workers. The lengthy timetable is necessary, EG&G officials believe, because the business might not be self-sustaining for some time. A competent black management team cannot be built up overnight. They also reckon it will be some years before employees can accumulate sufficient capital to buy a large share of the venture. As the business prospered, the price of a share would normally be expected to climb. And EG&G does not want to let the community down by prematurely selling a "piece of the action" when things are still in the sink-or-swim stage.

Unlike EG&G and Aerojet-General, most companies are unprepared to give serious thought to divestiture arrangements. Apart from occasional anti-trust actions, which force divestiture under anti-monopoly laws, the concept of divestiture runs counter to normal business practice. Divestitures of failing businesses are not unusual. But if a risky investment proves successful, especially in the inhospitable ghetto environment, companies expect to reap the benefits for their shareholders.

How soon companies can turn a profit in their ghetto operations will determine whether the back-to-the-city movement gathers steam or languishes. Early returns, while sparse, indicate the road to profitability will be a a long and hard one. Assessing the prospects for ghetto plants in a spring 1968 issue of the *Harvard Business Review,* John T. Garrity of McKinsey and Company flatly predicts they will lose money without government aid in the form of tax incentives, low-cost loans, or even operating subsidies. Fred J. Borch, chairman of General Electric Co. which has considerable experience in inner-city manufacturing, agrees. "Ghetto plants are high-risk operations." Mr. Borch cites "too many unknowns" and "conflicting viewpoints among the experts" as reasons why most major corporations will continue to take a lukewarm attitude toward inner-city manufacturing. Unless generous government incentives are made available to business, the executive doubts that the post-World War II exodus from the city will be reversed.

The ICBO Idea

Black ownership and management of business must spread from small, marginal stores in the inner city to major companies which can compete outside as well as inside the ghetto. Only then will the black man's role in the economy grow significantly.

This is the conviction of Darwin W. Bolden, national director of the ICBO (Interracial Council for Business Opportunity). The non-profit organization is one of the forerunners in the drive to bring the private sector's resources to bear on the problem of the minority businessman.

ICBO was founded in 1963 by a group of New York business and professional people, under the sponsorship of the Urban League and American Jewish Congress. Its aim is to break down what ICBO calls the "invisible wall" blocking the minority entrepreneur's entry into the mainstream of the economy. The major contribution of ICBO has been to mobilize the talents and energies of voluntary consultants in counseling struggling black businesses. The bulk of the effort has gone into showing minority entrepreneurs how to start and strengthen such modest businesses as grocery stores, beauty parlors, and radio and television shops. ICBO has more than 800 consultants on tap in six major cities—New York, St. Louis, Newark, Los Angeles, New Orleans, and Washington D.C. They gave a helping hand to 1,000 smaller inner-city businesses in 1967 and 1968. Volunteers serve as personal business consultants to ICBO clients in such vital areas as accounting, production, personnel, marketing, and financial planning.

On-the-job counseling alone, however, often falls short of meeting the ghetto businessman's needs. Consequently, ICBO has played a major role in opening up new credit sources, and sponsoring business education courses for minority businessmen.

The organization's newest thrust, says Mr. Bolden, is to develop black-owned banks, motels, supermarkets, and manufacturing plants on a wider scale. The lawyer and former civil rights worker asserts that only such sizeable enterprises—not a proliferation of "Mom and Pop" stores—are adequate vehicles for "economic empowerment" of black America. ICBO is shaping a "new enterprise" program designed to bring to fruition projects requiring capital of $100,000 or more. These bigger businesses would be able to break away from the segregated markets of the ghetto, and hopefully, be competitive in price, quality, and service with their white-owned counterparts. It plans to combine functions of a business broker, advisor, and underwriter in identifying, assessing, and helping to finance middle-sized businesses. Some businesses may be purchased from their white owners and transferred to black hands. While the shift in direction promises to strain the limited resources and staff of ICBO, it already has aided a few major undertakings.

On the west coast, 25 ICBO consultants sheparded a bright but inexperienced Negro engineer through the early stages of organizing his own firm. The product, an invention of his own, was a patented portable record player. The consultants aided in the negotiation of domestic and overseas patent agreements, developed marketing plans and opened doors to long-term financing. After 10 years of struggling, the young inventor now heads Cheeseboro Products, a company capitalized at over $500,000 that will eventually employ several hundred people.

Through ICBO efforts, $150,000 was raised for the Green Power Foundation, a non-profit economic development group in Los Angeles. The money went to a subsidiary making the "Watts Walloper" baseball bats. ICBO volunteers assisted in securing plant space, machinery, and negotiating a two-year pact with ash lumber suppliers in North Carolina. ICBO arranged the $1 million financing package which enabled a group of black businessmen to purchase a radio station in St. Louis. It is advising New Dimensions Publishing Co., a black-owned enterprise specializing in elementary school texts on African history and culture, on how to organize a national marketing program. Through its banking contacts, ICBO arranged a revolving line of credit for New Dimensions. The publishing firm hoped to do $150,000 in sales in 1969.

Though most of the new enterprises aided by ICBO will be black owned, the organization is just as eager to promote joint ventures with major corporations. In the works is a $6 million Harlem motel in which the Hotel Corporation of America will be a leading participant. Most of the shares in the motel company are to be sold within the Harlem community.

ICBO's local councils work closely with the SBA and banks to open credit lines for minority business. Sometimes, just the commitment to provide a consulting team paves the way for a bank loan to a client. In the 18 months ending June 30, 1968, small business loans arranged for clients exceeded $1.5 million.

Since ICBO has little money of its own to lend, new techniques have been devised to meet the chronic capital shortage from which most of its ghetto clients suffer. One of the most promising is the loan guarantee fund. Working with four New York banks, ICBO has formed a $730,000 loan guarantee fund in the soft loan area. Each dollar in the fund generates $4 in bank loans. ICBO assumes 50 per cent of the risk while the lending bank risks the other half. Each borrower must agree to maintain a consulting relationship until the loan is repaid.

Finding competent volunteer consultants is not always a key problem. But insuring an effective counseling relationship often is. In some cases the client holds misconceptions or exaggerated expectations about the consultant's role, and the consultant, typically a middle class white, is often not sensitized to the special problems of running a ghetto business. While technically capable as an accountant or engineer, the consultant may not be able to bridge the cultural gap and establish a rapport with the client.

To reduce the chances of failure in a counseling relationship, hard experience has taught ICBO several lessons:

1. Make an in-depth analysis of a potential client's business, getting an unsentimental appraisal from a panel of consultants. The panel usually includes an accountant, lawyer, and a banker. The organization always seeks advice from someone who has made good in the same field and knows the ropes.
2. Maintain close liaison with the client through a consulting team. Although it is not always possible to assign more than one consultant to a client, ICBO favors the team approach for reasons of continuity. A sharing of insights into the client's problems is helpful as well.
3. Stress consistent follow-up and the filing of regular reports on client's progress. To achieve this, ICBO has found it necessary to develop an experienced supervisory staff, both to monitor clients and to check up on the consultants. The ratio of volunteers to professional staff is about 50 to 1.
4. Work with outside groups which can tap a variety of business skills at little cost. In New York City, for example, ICBO has received enthusiastic support from the Harvard Business School Alumni Club, Chase Manhattan Bank, and the Young Presidents Organization.
5. Avoid undertaking short-term "rescue" operations for business in trouble. One of ICBO's tenets is to insist on a comprehensive attack on a client's problems, not just a hasty crash program.

6. Balance experience with youth. Many young consultants are able to put in long hours in ironing out their client's financial or production problems. Others, particularly those holding top management slots, may be more useful for their "clout and contacts."

Besides their counseling activities, ICBO local affiliates sponsor business education seminars to upgrade clients' skills. The free courses, which more than 1,500 have attended, cover such essential topics as bookkeeping, advertising, and business law. In Newark alone, about 400 enrolled in ICBO sponsored classes in an effort to rebuild their businesses after the July 1967 riots.

To combat the negative view many teenagers hold toward business careers, several councils have attempted to give the youngsters an inside picture of business life. Holding field trips to factories, and sponsoring Junior Achievement chapters are two activities that have met with some success.

ICBO is rapidly adding new initiatives to its agenda. These include:

—raising $1 million for a venture capital fund with which to provide seed money for underwriting sizeable new businesses. In the past, a lack of capital resources has prevented ICBO from god-fathering many promising ventures.

—organizing two "poor people's" corporations, one rural and one urban, to process and distribute fortified foods. The project is financed by a $350,000 Office of Economic Opportunity grant.

Support for its $1 million annual operating budget comes from foundation grants, principally Ford and Rockefeller Foundation money. Corporate contributions, though still slender, are growing.

To widen the scope of its activities ICBO had launched a major drive to raise $3.5 million over the 1969–1971 period. The money would be used to more than double the number of local councils and permit an expansion of financing, education, and advisory services.

A Philadelphia Success Story

When Reverend Leon H. Sullivan rises to the pulpit of north Philadelphia's Zion Baptist Church, his parishioners are as likely to hear a sermon on the virtues of "economic emancipation" as on the evils of racism. A dynamic speaker with a towering 6 foot 5 inch frame, Sullivan is a tireless advocate of economic self-help measures as a way to break down the walls of the ghetto. "To have durable power, black men must develop economic power," he says. Once a black militant, Sullivan has earned a reputation as a forceful pragmatist with a successful formula for waging his private war on poverty. Starting with a converted jail cell in north Philadelphia in 1964, Sullivan has created a nationwide chain of more than 75 job training centers. Known as OICs (Opportunities Industrialization Centers), they constitute the nation's largest self-help group for the disadvantaged.

The OICs are geared to bolster trainee morale and motivation, as well as teach elementary job skills. Philadelphia's five centers alone have turned out more than 7,000 graduates, 90 per cent of whom were placed in jobs.

OIC's achievements on the job-training front led the energetic clergyman into a new direction—the promotion of community-owned black business enterprises. With an unusual entrepreneurial flair, Sullivan launched his first three profit-making ventures in rapid succession during the second half of 1968. In less than a year, the black community had parleyed an investment pool of about $250,000 into acquisition of $4 million worth of properties. All are black owned and managed and will plow a portion of their earnings into OIC and other non-profit projects for Negroes. Waving the "Progress" banner, Sullivan's companies—an aerospace firm, a garment maker, and a shopping plaza—are designed to prove that Negroes can compete, given the opportunity, with anyone and anywhere.

The initial venture, Progress Aerospace Enterprises (PAE) is an electronics firm spawned with a helping hand from the Missile and Space Division of General Electric. GE made available a handful of experienced black engineers and administrators. More important, GE insured PAE a flying start by giving the company a $2.6 million Air Force subcontract to make electronic components. GE took no remuneration for its technical assistance, which will continue through the "shakedown" phase.

To avoid the paternalistic tag attached to "captive" supplier relationships, PAE is developing a broad capability in the specialty electronics field. Within 6 months after starting operations, PAE won subcontracts from Boeing, Lockheed, and Western Electric.

The Reverend Sullivan considers the aerospace project as a proving ground to show Negroes can run a profitable company in a highly technical and demanding field. It will employ 160 Negroes, most of them hard-core unemployed, along with a few experienced white technicians. A $522,000 Labor Department manpower grant will defray training costs.

Progress Garment Manufacturing Co. is the first in a proposed group of black owned apparel-making factories, employing many ghetto women who might otherwise be on welfare. The Villager, one of the nation's largest women's garment makers, ushered Sullivan into the apparel field by negotiating a sizeable contract for women's separates.

Singer Company designed the factory layout and provided a battery of sewing machines at a substantial discount. It plans to open an affiliated child care center to ease the burden for working mothers. Progress Garment markets a proprietary apparel line under the "Ten-Thirty-Six Fashions" label. In 1970, sales may reach the $1 million level.

When planning new projects, Sullivan is not afraid to talk with the "establishment," seeking money and advice. His self-help theme, backed by an impressive track record with the OIC has solidified his business support. White businessmen find themselves captivated by Sullivan's charismatic quality, his practical bent, and his eloquent support of private enterprise. Frequent speeches, sprinkled with such effective homilies as "you can't integrate the suburbs with relief checks" and "integration without preparation is frustration" always stress the positive aspects of what "green power" can accomplish for the black community.

An Industrial Advisory Committee, comprised of heads of blue chip corporations such as Coca-Cola and Boeing, is a big asset in raising money and opening doors in high places. One of Sullivan's staunchest supporters is First Pennsylvania Banking and Trust Co., which provided a $1.6 million loan to finance Progress Plaza.

Dedicated in November 1968, Progress Plaza is a new $1.7 million shopping center in a slum neighborhood of Philadelphia near Temple University. Each of the sixteen stores, including the branch of a major Philadelphia bank, is managed by Negroes. Several are black-managed branches of major national retail chains. The Plaza draws Negro shoppers from all parts of the city, and is an unquestioned hit. Ten of the shops are owned by Negroes, many of whom were never proprietors before. The shops run the gamut from dry cleaning to men's wear.

Although Sullivan continues to irk some members of the Philadelphia business community with "Buy Black" pronouncements, he is no longer the thorn in the flesh he used to be. Before founding OIC, Sullivan led 400 Negro ministers in a massive consumer boycott campaign against some of the city's largest companies. Sullivan claims the sustained effort "broke down the system of discrimination against colored workers in Philadelphia."

Unlike some black militants, Sullivan does not equate "black capitalism" with separatism. Separatism is self-defeating, he insists. He likes to speak of the "All-American road to prosperity," and insists black-owned business can flourish "downtown" as well as in the ghetto. His "Progress" enterprises, while geared primarily to develop black capital and managerial skills, are operated on an integrated basis.

In all his ventures Sullivan maintains the principle of community ownership by raising seed money in his own back yard. The OICs were launched by numerous contributions totaling $40,000 from among Sullivan's 4,000 parishioners. Sullivan chipped in by mortgaging his own home. Later, 650 church members, under Sullivan's direction, organized Zion Investment Associates, a holding company that put up the initial capital for his profit-making endeavors. To draw parishioners into the investment program, Sullivan devised a mutual-fund-like "10-36 Plan." Each subscriber pledges $10 a month over a 36 month period. To establish PAE, for example, the investor group raised $200,000 on the installment plan. Another $300,000 came from a First Pennsylvania Banking and Trust Co. loan. To expand Zion's ownership base further, Sullivan recently invited 20 other Negro ministers to ask their parishioners to buy shares on the 10-36 Plan. The response was immediate—4,000 subscribers signed up within a three month period. At the beginning of 1969, after a temporary cut-off in new subscribers there was a waiting list of some 10,000 potential investors.

Because the investment projects materialized so fast, the program "captured the spirit of the black community," says Elmer Young, Reverend Sullivan's right hand man. Yet prospective investors, few of whom know the difference between a bond and a stock, are warned against "overoptimism." Otherwise, they might become disappointed over what are likely to be slender financial returns in the near future. "We tell them it's an act of faith," Mr. Young remarks, "and not a 'get-rich-quick' scheme."

The note of caution is well-advised. Zion Investment plans to distribute only two-fifths of the profits from its enterprises to investors. One-fifth will go to employees in profit-sharing plans and the remaining two-fifths will be plowed back into a non-profit charitable trust.

The Zion Charitable Trust was set up as a self-perpetuating umbrella for Sullivan's non-taxable ghetto improvement activities. It sponsors college scholarships, initiates low-income housing projects, and recently opened an entrepreneurial training center for black businessmen. In September 1968, the trust received a shot in the arm from a sizeable ($700,000) Ford Foundation grant. Besides the entrepreneurial school, the funds will help finance feasibility studies for new business ventures, and technical assistance to small Negro businesses. Ford's confidence in Sullivan's brand of economic bootstrapping was expressed in another way as well.

Under a new policy of making "program-related investments," aside from its regular grants, Ford invested $300,000 in Progress Enterprises, a new profit-making arm of Zion. Ford, whose investment is convertible into non-voting common stock, will have little voice in how the money is spent. "It's a bet on Leon Sullivan," noted a Ford Foundation official. With the Ford money, Sullivan has the makings of a "venture capital" company with considerable borrowing leverage.

For the first time, Sullivan has a capability of putting together "package deals" encompassing job training, manufacturing, and shopping centers. He sees the OIC as a "vestibule" to provide the semi-skilled labor for his industrial enterprises. The immediate challenge, however, is to acquire the black managerial talent to staff his burgeoning enterprises. To meet the problem, Sullivan has set up an economic development center, which in its first year will turn out a cadre of at least 40 "economic developers." The graduates will concentrate on developing shopping centers in ghettos around the country. Once sites are picked, Progress Enterprises will be the financing vehicle, drawing on banks and insurance companies for long-term mortgages. Eventually Progress Enterprises plans to spin off the shopping centers to local black business groups.

Minority Entrepreneurship in Rochester

In Rochester's inner city, ownership of small business is gradually shifting to the people who live there. Not dramatically, but nonetheless noticeably, the fight for economic survival is getting easier among Rochester's black self-employed.

Since the beginning of 1968, Rochester's 45,000 minority group members have seen an increasing number of their neighbors go into business for themselves, expand their stores, or buy out existing white merchants. While most of the 40-odd new ventures involve retail goods and services, a handful are more ambitious, and include contracting, camera repair, and plastic molding.

Playing a leading role in promoting new independent businesses in the ghetto is a small but effective community development organization, the RBOC (Rochester Business Opportunities Corporation). Supported by more than 60 Rochester Corporations, RBOC is a non-profit agency devoted to "giving the minority entrepreneurs a change," according to RBOC president William J. Maxion. It brings a wide range of financing and counseling services to the aspiring entrepreneur.

The initial impetus for RBOC grew out of the racial tensions which gripped Rochester following the 1964 riots. In the aftermath of the riots, Eastman Kodak became embroiled in a running battle with a militant black group, FIGHT, over its minority hiring and training policies. Once the controversy over jobs was resolved, FIGHT pressed Kodak to establish a large community-owned plant in the inner city. FIGHT suggested as a model the Watts Manufacturing Company, established in Los Angeles by Aerojet-General. Kodak demurred, arguing that such an approach had less relevance to Rochester. The ghetto unemployment rate was much lower and transportation to jobs not as critical a problem as in Watts. Rochester firms were already hard at work in a cooperative endeavor to employ the hard-core.

As an alternative, Kodak proposed a small business development corporation, financed primarily by large firms but managed with the help of inner-city businessmen. Its plan, Kodak said, "reflects a feeling that independence, dignity, and opportunity more than jobs are needed at this time." To avoid the taint of white paternalism, Kodak said such a corporation should not limit itself to a few dependent, subsidiary-type operations. Very quickly, other Rochester firms embraced the Kodak plan, and RBOC was started.

When RBOC's 3-man staff first opened shop in early 1968, explained former general manager John L. Blake, "we thought in terms of new factories and lots of jobs." Much to the surprise of Blake, those who streamed in asking for assistance were primarily small ghetto merchants of the "Mom-and-Pop" store variety—dry cleaners, grocers, beauty parlor and service station operators. Others were interested in moving into lines with greater expansion potential, such as construction sub-contracting and trucking. Most had financial problems and lacked know-how in critical areas such as selling, accounting or purchasing.

RBOC felt it could not ignore a host of potentially able, but inexperienced and undercapitalized black entrepreneurs. While Kodak at the outset had agreed to help launch four small inner-city industrial firms, RBOC realized that similar new projects could take many months to put together. Mr. Blake pointed out that small retailers have "high visibility" in the inner city, even if they do not provide many jobs. If the "little man" was spurned while RBOC waited for larger projects to unfold, a damaging credibility gap might be opened in the black community. RBOC's 28-man Board of Trustees —most of them executives with Rochester firms—did not want to let this happen.

A sampling of RBOC sponsored firms shows the diversity of their operations.

An auto body repairman with a steady clientele lacked indoor workspace during the winter months. This limited his business potential. RBOC arranged a $25,000 loan from the SBA. The funds are being used to enlarge the repairman's shop.

A dry cleaning store operator wanted to expand, but lacked the capital. Consultants recruited by RBOC provided temporary accounting help, advised on relocation of the plant, and suggested the owner seek a $55,000 bank loan. After RBOC put up $10,000 and an SBA guarantee was given, the bank loan was approved. With a new cleaning plant, the owner has been able to move into the industrial dry cleaning field.

Kodak agreed to sponsor a thermo-plastic parts business in the inner city. A Negro chemist, a former Kodak employee, took on the project with a personal investment of $5,000. Kodak provided him with a tailor-made course in the technical aspects of the plastics business. RBOC put together the financial package, including a $75,000 bank loan with SBA guarantee.

While Kodak provides a sheltered market initially, the five-man operation is preparing to meet other customer requirements as well. The firm's five-year goal is to have 20 employees with $600,000 a year in sales.

RBOC's largest commitment is FIGHTON, Inc., a new $600,000 manufacturing company organized by FIGHT with the help of Xerox. It will make vacuum cleaners, metal stampings, and transformers for Xerox's internal use.

Besides purchasing most of the output in the first two years, Xerox will offer free technical and managerial support. To get the venture off the ground, RBOC is spending over $200,000 to acquire and renovate a plant to lease to FIGHTON. RBOC is also pledged to help find customers other than Xerox to eventually put the business on a more independent footing.

The FIGHTON project was the climax of almost four years of collaboration between the black self-help organization and Xerox on job training programs for the disadvantaged. "It took us a year and a half before we were laughing at the same jokes," recalls Minister Franklin D. R. Florence, of FIGHT. "You can not wave a magic wand and say 'black capitalism' and expect it to be as easy as that."

In screening applicants, RBOC tries to eliminate those with dim prospects. It does not want to foster "hot-house" businesses which might collapse once RBOC loans and advice are withdrawn. Of primary importance is a careful assessment of the individual entrepreneur's aptitude for running an independent operation. To strengthen incentives RBOC requires would-be businessmen to put up equity of their own wherever possible. If a venture, such as the Kodak-sponsored camera repair center, is large enough RBOC suggests a profit-sharing or stock-option plan for employees.

Beyond that, RBOC's Business Development Committee takes a close look at the market potential of the goods or service, the growth opportunities, and the likelihood of long-term profitability. It discourages capital-intensive or highly technical projects unless there is a commitment from a major company to provide training, technical advice, and guarantee a market for the product. Of the more than two dozen RBOC-sponsored firms launched in 1968, only three had the benefit of long-term sales contracts with major Rochester firms. "It's tough to find companies who are willing to provide a guaranteed market for a brand-new supplier," said Mr. Maxion.

Although it has had mixed results so far, RBOC continues to urge established industry to give new inner-city enterprises a lift-off through long-term purchase contracts. It does not view a guaranteed market as a permanent subsidy, but rather as a way to overcome the start-up hurdles until other purchasers are found. To the extent that any subsidy exists, it comes through the provision of free technical assistance to the producer from the purchaser or from RBOC.

As a matter of policy, financial aid and business counseling go hand-in-hand. From its own capital pool of $250,000, the corporation makes loans, loan guarantees, and sometimes equity investments. Loan terms are typically flexible, and RBOC takes risks that banks are unable to take. Stock investments, few of which have exceeded $5,000, are intended to keep a promising business from being too heavily saddled with debt. Thus, RBOC often supplies the missing link in a financing package.

Often, RBOC volunteers have taken a potentially good idea and translated it into a feasibility study that might whet a lender's interest.

For technical advice, RBOC relies on a roster of specialists in accounting, marketing, and production who volunteer their services. A local CPA group, the Harvard Business School Association, and other volunteers from among the major companies in the area, provide an ample reservoir of talent and experience. To make the counseling effort more effective, volunteers watch the fledgling firms carefully so they can anticipate problems.

As many minority businessmen have only an elementary knowledge of bookkeeping and finance, some of the most valuable inputs have come from Rochester CPAs. They assist entrepreneurs in formulating "bankable" proposals and help them keep their books once they are in operation.

A key to RBOC's ability to get results, admits Mr. Maxion, is the dedication of the 28-man Board of Trustees, and their widespread influence in the city. Most are top executives of nationally known firms such as General Dynamics, Xerox, and Gannet Co. Yet they participate personally in all of RBOC's deliberations. Rochester's banking fraternity is also actively represented on the Board.

One weakness of RBOC, according to some observers, is the lack of formal links with non-business minority groups, such as the FIGHT organization or the Urban League. This has given rise to occasional charges of RBOC being dominated by "corporate giants." RBOC supporters on the other hand argue that the presence of nine minority entrepreneurs on the Board is a guarantee that minority group points of view have a channel for expression.

Taking stock after the one year, William Maxion calls RBOC's impact on minority business opportunities "encouraging." More than $1,500,000 of investment money has flowed to the ghetto from local banks, the SBA and RBOC. FIGHTON alone accounts for about $500,000 of the new funds. In their first year of operation RBOC-sponsored firms are expected to chalk up sales of about $3.5 million. "Money is no longer the big problem," says Mr. Maxion.

In 1969, RBOC had assurances of another $250,000 from its corporate supporters and was planning to draw additional funds from churches and civic organizations. If the money is adequate, there is nevertheless a shortage of capable entrepreneurs to implement a growing number of interesting business proposals.

Several, such as a bookbindery, were generated from RBOC requests that companies examine their purchasing habits to see if any new inner-city source might be added. This is an area where RBOC is hopeful much more can be done.

Another problem is assuring the success of the new ventures once the initial injections of money and advice have been absorbed. RBOC expects some of the new businesses will be a flop, but the percentage should be far lower than the national average for small business.

Even at this early stage, RBOC has received warm accolades from federal officials and national business organizations. The United States Chamber of Commerce stated that RBOC "shows a pattern worthy of close observation by leaders of other urban areas who want to open opportunities for inner-city people to become self-employed and genuinely part of the economic mainstream." Several other cities are modeling community development corporations after the Rochester plan.

Conclusion

The four different approaches toward fostering black-owned business discussed in this chapter are certainly not the only ones being tried. Yet they represent several possible "models," each with its own advantages and disadvantages.

The ghetto plant, provided it holds out the possibility of ownership to the black community somewhere along the line, seems perhaps the most promising approach for establishing sizeable black businesses. It may be the only way to rapidly create "green power" among black employees as well as provide a mechanism for training black managers.

If black capitalism is going to have a material impact on the ghetto, most experts agree it will have to be with black firms employing 25 to 500 employees. The traditional trades, the small retail and service store, have a high rate of failure and typically accumulate little capital for their owners. The economic multiplier effect of one business employing 200 people is far greater than one hundred businesses employing two men each.

So far only a small number of major corporations have been willing to set up ghetto "spin-offs" who may have to be nursed along for several years before attaining self-sufficiency.

The main drawbacks, as industrialists see them, are the uncertain advantages of a ghetto plant, the delicate problems involved in yielding technical direction and ownership, and the issue of how to finance the transfer of ownership on other than a give-away basis.

These are problems that have to be met and solved in due course. Meanwhile there are bold beginnings to be made, and the experience of Rochester with the RBOC, for example, shows what a tightly knit white business community can do in a short period of time.

Index

The American Assembly

COLUMBIA UNIVERSITY

About the American Assembly

The American Assembly was established by Dwight D. Eisenhower at Columbia University in 1950. It holds nonpartisan meetings and publishes authoritative books to illuminate issues of United States policy.

An affiliate of Columbia, with offices in the Graduate School of Business, the Assembly is a national, educational institution incorporated in the State of New York.

The Assembly seeks to provide information, stimulate discussion, and evoke independent conclusions in matters of vital public interest.

AMERICAN ASSEMBLY SESSIONS

At least two national programs are initiated each year. Authorities are retained to write background papers presenting essential data and defining the main issues in each subject.

About 60 men and women representing a broad range of experience. competence, and American leadership meet for several days to discuss the Assembly topic and consider alternatives for national policy.

All Assemblies follow the same procedure. The background papers are sent to participants in advance of the Assembly. The Assembly meets in small groups for four or five lengthy periods. All groups use the same agenda. At the close of these informal sessions participants adopt in plenary session a final report of findings and recommendations.

Regional, state, and local Assemblies are held following the national session at Arden House. Assemblies have also been held in England, Switzerland, Malaysia, Canada, the Caribbean, South America, the Philippines, and Japan. Over one hundred institutions have co-sponsored one or more Assemblies.

ARDEN HOUSE

Home of the American Assembly and scene of the national sessions is Arden House, which was given to Columbia University in 1950 by W. Averell Harriman. E. Roland Harriman joined his brother in contributing toward adaptation of the property for conference purposes. The buildings and surrounding land, known as the Harriman Campus of Columbia University, are 50 miles north of New York City.

Arden House is a distinguished conference center. It is self-supporting and operates throughout the year for use by organizations with educational objectives. The American Assembly is a tenant of this Columbia University facility only during Assembly sessions.

AMERICAN ASSEMBLY BOOKS

The background papers for each Assembly program are published in cloth and paperbound editions for use by individuals, libraries, businesses, public agencies, non-governmental organizations, educational institutions, discussion and service groups. In this way the deliberations of Assembly sessions are continued and extended.

The subjects of Assembly programs to date are:

1951 — United States-Western Europe Relationships
1952 — Inflation
1953 — Economic Security for Americans
1954 — The United States' Stake in the United Nations
— The Federal Government Service
1955 — United States Agriculture
— The Forty-Eight States
1956 — The Representation of the United States Abroad
— The United States and the Far East
1957 — International Stability and Progress
— Atoms for Power
1958 — The United States and Africa
— United States Monetary Policy
1959 — Wages, Prices, Profits, and Productivity
— The United States and Latin America
1960 — The Federal Government and Higher Education
— The Secretary of State
— Goals for Americans
1961 — Arms Control: Issues for the Public
— Outer Space: Prospects for Man and Society
1962 — Automation and Technological Change
— Cultural Affairs and Foreign Relations
1963 — The Population Dilemma
— The United States and the Middle East
1964 — The United States and Canada
— The Congress and America's Future
1965 — The Courts, the Public, and the Law Explosion
— The United States and Japan
1966 — State Legislatures in American Politics
— A World of Nuclear Powers?
— The United States and the Philippines
— Challenges to Collective Bargaining
1967 — The United States and Eastern Europe
— Ombudsmen for American Government?
1968 — Uses of the Seas

— Law in a Changing America
— Overcoming World Hunger
1969 — Black Economic Development
— The Role of the States in the Urban Crisis